HARD RAIN/ SLOW TRAIN

Passages About Dylan

MICHAEL ANTON MILLER

Jupiter Hollow Media, LLC

Copyright © 2011 Michael Anton Miller

Published by Jupiter Hollow Media LLC
Denver, Colorado

All rights reserved

Chapter Three first appeared in
Journal for Anthroposophy,
Summer, 1988, Number 47,
and was reprinted
in the anthology,
The Riddle of America,
edited by John Wulsin, (AWSNA,2001)

Back Cover Art by Frank Miller

ISBN-10: 0578052660
EAN-13: 9780578052663

It was not only the ecstasy of his flaming hymns, which in that revolutionary time incidentally acquired some qualities of a manifesto: it was above all the person of the poet, the air of noble idealism and exalted transcendence that produced so deep an effect in this period of profound corruption and hopeless commitment to material ends.
— Hermann Hesse, "On Holderlin".

Rock music, the authentic mark or banner of counterculture, is something that once was a new variety of indigenous American religion, however brief or secular, momentarily akin to the outflarings that have engendered permanent beliefs among us: Mormonism, Pentecostalism, Adventism. The moment passed, probably in the winter of 1969-1970, when spiritual intensity was at a brief height....

The failure of rock criticism, except of a purely technical sort, is another indication of the retreat from intelligence in the purported counterculture.
— Harold Bloom, *Omens Of Millennium*.

Nota bene:
The customary historical usage of the pronoun "he" to personify the human being generically is a matter of linguistic convenience only.

CONTENTS

PREFACE 1
A Stranger In A Strange Land..9

1: Ironic Points...11
2: Dylanfolk 15
3: The Thief Who Kindly Spoke...19
4: From A Chrome Horse Falling 29
5: The Explosion The Night Watchman Saw 41
6: Come In, She Said...53

HIGHER ROCKS: A TRANSCENDENTAL INTERLUDE..71

7: The Return Of The Feminine 89
8: Bob Dylan's Blues And The Twin Goddess 111
9: Journey Through Dark Heat...135
10: Far From The Turbulent Space......................................161
11: Where The Swift Don't Win The Race 179
12: Make Room, Then, For The Life-Giving Ones.............203

Coda: Lifting The Veil, (If Only A Little)........................215
Discography 253
Bibliography 255

PREFACE

> Pay attention to the poet,
> You need him and you know it.
>
> - Bruce Cockburn: "Maybe The Poet," 1982

This book pays attention to the poet in Bob Dylan. The genius we know by that name includes the poet but cannot be delimited by that designation. It's too multifaceted for such a straight-jacket. And yet, what would Dylan be without the poet in him? One more singer and songwriter? Another talented performer? He is all those things, of course, and also something more. The genius known as Bob Dylan is a rare and perhaps new kind of flowering, but the stem, right down to the root of it, is the poet.

Geniuses are like Rorschach tests. We can't help seeing in them that which we see, because we are who we are. It's not a matter of wanting to pin the man down, adding another dead butterfly to our collection. It's more a matter of getting to know ourselves better by understanding what this new flowering can mean for us and to us.

The poet in Dylan, like any poet, lives and dies by his words and by his particular way of using them. And so the attention paid to the poet in Dylan, as found in *Hard Rain/Slow Train*, focuses on the words and on the way they are used, not as a way of trapping the poet but as a way of suggesting the incredible and astonishing patterns of his flight, which is like the magical and mesmerizing flight of a butterfly. The sight of a butterfly on the wing thrills the heart.

Cockburn's right, we *do* need the poet. We need him because he represents us better than we do ourselves. Our deep need for expression, which Ralph Waldo Emerson called "our painful secret," finds a larger degree of fulfillment in his achievement than we have so far managed on our own. As Emerson noted, a man is only half himself, the other half is his expression. We look to the poet as the one whose expression comes closest to our own, had we a like power to impart it.

Our encounter with the poet can have a deeply spiritual effect on us, profoundly enlarging our awareness of ourselves. Emerson aptly characterized the spiritual nature of that encounter perhaps better than anyone else, when he wrote:

> With what joy I begin to read a poem, which I confide in as an inspiration! And now my chains are to be broken; I shall mount above these clouds and opaque airs in which I live, – opaque, though they seem transparent, – and from the heaven of truth I shall see and comprehend my relations. That will reconcile me to life, and renovate nature, to see trifles animated by a tendency, and to know what I am doing. Life will no more be noise; now I shall see men and women, and know the signs by which they may be discerned from fools and satans. This day shall be better than my birthday: then I became an animal: now I am invited into the science of the real.

Our encounter with the poet can be so deeply and totally transformative that it could almost be considered a rebirth. At least that is the case when it affects us in a way that reconciles us to life and renovates nature, so that we are better able to know what we are doing. The poet, as Emerson envisioned him, is not the man "of poetical talents, or of industry and skill in metres," but rather the true poet, whose "sign and credentials are, that he announces that which no man foretold. He is the true and only doctor; he knows and he tells; he is the only teller of news, for he was present and privy to the appearance which he describes."

In the view that is developed in this book, Bob Dylan is such a teller of news. The new appearance, which he has been present and privy to, and which he has been at pains to describe with his art, is this: the growing recognition that our inner life, our authentic and existential life, resides fundamentally in the dynamic interplay of self and mind and in the often dramatic conflicts that arise out of that dynamic as we struggle to find true love – or perhaps better said, as we strive to discover the truth of love, which is only realizable through conscious transcendence of that duality.

It is an integral part of Dylan's genius to have recognized that our ordinary longing to find love in the world by connecting up with a significant other, which plays such a central role in our emotional life and development, parallels the more profound longing of the human spirit for self-realization. Ordinary love songs, which have ever been the stuff of popular music, give expression to the constant longing of the individual to find love. Traditionally, a typical love song narrates some aspect of the joys and the difficulties a person experiences, once he has become involved in the never-ending battle of the sexes, in his effort to find love. As such, ordinary love-songs frequently have the soap-opera quality of melodrama.

In Dylan's art, the form of the love song is employed to reveal the intense drama of our authentic inner life where we are constantly striving to discover and comprehend the mystery of our existence. This deeper struggle also involves the mysteries of sexual dynamics, but on the more intimate plane of personal consciousness. Having observed the intimate and acutely personal interplay of the self and mind in terms of the male and female aspects of consciousness, Dylan had the genius to express that deeper struggle by artistically elaborating its particular raptures and disappointments in a manner that mirrors the ardent language and aspirations of conventional love songs.

And this is what makes Dylan's art so exquisitely intimate, that a person's observation of this inner private drama can never be subjected to ordinary logical criticism and discourse. It is not in any way an objective affair upon which anyone else has a right to comment. This points to another integral aspect of Dylan's genius, which he expressed in the line: "It ain't no use a-talkin' to me/It's just the same as talking to you." That line is from the 1964 song, "I Shall Be Free No. 10." Fast-forward 42 years to the 2006 album, *Modern Times* and listen to the song, "Ain't Talkin'." With its oft-repeated line, "Ain't talkin', just walkin'," he is essentially saying, "I haven't been talking at all, if talking means speaking to others. I've been speaking only to myself in my songs, which has only been my way of getting on in the world, my way of walking through this life." A Dylan song is therefore best understood as an artistic rendering of an extremely intimate self-conversation.

In the point of view developed in this book, the "I" or self is understood as representing the masculine factor in personal consciousness, which primarily manifests through the will, as individual existential self-assertion. On the other hand, the mind is taken to represent the feminine factor in which the thoughts of the self are continually conceived and given form.

Those are the two sides of our consciousness, and both are needed for thoughts to arise in consciousness where we can see them. And when love enters into the process, there is a greater likelihood that the fertility of the mind will produce fruit that is both attractive and vitally wholesome.

An accurate observation of the subtle and intimate interactions of self and mind can only be achieved from a point of view that transcends the essential duality of self and mind, which is to say, from a perspective that is already inherently transcendental. The ever-present "I" in a Dylan lyric is not primarily the limited "I" of any specific given individual. Rather, it is the existential "I" that is fundamentally the same in each of us. The existential "I," as the formless and essentially unknowable *one* in us, is that aspect of our being that is inherently capable of perceiving all possible forms that make up *the many*. By reason of the existential "I," each of us is instantaneously involved in the high eternal mystery of The One and The Many that lies at the heart of existence and that constitutes "the quick" of life.

In contrast to the existential "I," there is the mind with its mysterious and infinite capacity to conceive and give form to the thoughts that continually stream out of the self. Those thoughts, until they have entered the living fertility of the mind, can only live intuitively in the self as mere seeds or impulses of potential life. The self needs the mind to give life and form to its intuitions if the self is to behold its own thoughts, and through that beholding, realize its existential reality.

The analysis and explication of Dylan's lyrics in this book derive from an exploration of these two overriding aspects of his genius and art. One, that his songs are essentially self-conversations that, artistically formed into riddles, memorialize the inner events of spiritual transformation. And two, that the spiritual striving for the realization of love, as the primary, procreant urge of life, extends into the transcendental realm of our deep existential reality as an intimate affair of the heart, where the wedded bliss of a harmoniously united mind and self can discover the integrity of its true spiritual being.

As the self needs the mind to give life and substance to its intuitions, so the mind needs the self, one that is upright and firmly charged with true and faithful intuitions. The mind, like outer nature, which is its cosmic analog, is essentially pure fertility, and its inherent power to bestow life and form to any and all life-impulses tends to run wild if left unchecked. A mind without a self could only be a chaos. A self without a mind, on the other hand, is completely unthinkable and would be absolutely meaningless. If life is to have any meaning, it can only be for a self.

The mind can often be a troublesome aspect in the life of consciousness until the individual has achieved transcendence within his being. Until then, it is very much the case for the existential "I" that, as Dylan expressed it on *Modern Times*, "Ain't nothing more depressing than trying to satisfy this woman of mine." At the same time, the existential "I" can also be problematic in the struggle to achieve inner harmony of self and mind. It is only from a steadfast love of truth in the self, which is like a metaphysical sac housing the intuitive seeds of life, that the power to transform the mind can come.

The enduring fire of desire emanating from the central point in any person's being is his metaphysical masculinity, which secretly longs to see the fruit of that life come alive as realized creations in the world, as the living and life-giving offspring of his individual existence. With that central masculine side of his being, a person reaches out to the innate and infinite fertility of the mind, to his metaphysical femininity, within the inviolable intimacy of the heart. From the heart, the masculine side of being burns with the love of truth, and from the feminine side with the truth of love, without which no form can come to life. When the mind has been impregnated with the spermatic intuitions of the self in the spirit of love, "she" can bestow the form of life upon them in that same spirit.

With the conscious awakening to the love of truth at the core of his being, the self recognizes the mind as his essential helpmate in his deep desire for self-realization. With this recognition, she is transformed for him into that incomparable and enduring beauty who continually renews the desire of his heart, because she is the only one capable of giving life and substance to his deepest intuitions. This love of the awakened self for the mind elevates her into the high point of femininity within human consciousness, which transforms her into the active soul, whose fertility is capable of creating the new. At the same time, the existential "I," now transformed into the transcendental self, is conscious of what he is doing. No wonder Bob Dylan has repeatedly and insistently claimed that he is a *conscious* artist.

Such, then, are the metaphysical perspectives that inform the Passages About Dylan in *Hard Rain/Slow Train*.

A Stranger In A Strange Land

Suppose you were born to be a great creative artist but because you grew up in the USA in the 1940s and '50s surrounded by the Wasteland (not the intellectual, literary perception of it but the actual milieu itself), and your young eyes, fired by the unconscious and perhaps karmic urge for greatness, looked out over the weary world searching for at least an echo of the wondrous and mysterious, and yes sacred, life pulsing at the heart of your being until finally upon the cold and barren plains you saw as though darkly through a glass that something *was* moving, that something *did* seem to be alive.

Suppose that what you saw was what people called popular music – black music, folk music and rock and roll. God was dead, people said, if not with words then with the way they lived as though the soul were merely an accident of biological machinery; but not for you, you saw this music not just as it was but shimmering with possibilities and, like sunlight calling forth buried seeds, it called forth your peculiar talents. Suppose you got a guitar from Sears and Roebuck on your 10th birthday and quickly learned to play and soon you began to sing and to write your own songs. But somehow it wouldn't come right. They were rock and roll songs all right but they were not *your* songs. Driven by the need to fulfill your destiny, you continued in the face of confusions and hardships until you realized it is easy to do rock and roll songs but it is hard to do *your* songs, songs that say what you want to say, the way you want to say it.

Suppose that, lo and behold, others seemed to like *your* songs – though to judge by what they said they didn't understand really just what you were trying to say with your songs. No matter, you go on writing them and singing them and the truer they were the more people seemed to misunderstand, but they liked them anyway – apparently for their own reasons.

Suppose that by-and-by you became famous and people started calling you the champion of *their* ideas, making you into a legendary spokesman for mass-movements and believing that you somehow had answers for them, and that all this sold records but also set up false expectations so that as you continued doing what you'd always done, that is, *expressing your own inner being as artistically as you could,* people started eventually lashing out and berating you for betraying them. How could they not have understood by now that your business was being true to the guidance of your own intuitions?

Suppose you learned to accept all this and after a while figured it was just your fate so you might as well go on with it, making the music, making the songs and just let people go on making of them what they will. Suppose *your creative journey through the world remained a personal and private thing* deepening and renewing your own existence, while its effects upon audiences were various and strangely incongruent. Suppose you went on, like all real artists, making your art as the years advanced and that the work somehow continued to prolong and extend your fame, but as always, *still* for all the wrong reasons.

1

IRONIC POINTS

> Yet, dotted everywhere
> Ironic points of light
> Flash out wherever the Just
> Exchange their messages...
>
> -W.H. Auden

"Only that which does not teach," wrote William Butler Yeats, "which does not cry out, which does not persuade, which does not explain, is irresistible." Perhaps this is why I still find Bob Dylan and his work, after all these years, so irresistible. His songs, considered a kind of poetry, neither seek to teach nor persuade, and most certainly they do not seek to explain. They do, however, in a certain sense "cry out." But this has to do with the fact that his work stems from an oral tradition and also with the nature of his chosen medium: rock and roll. Ironically enough, the choice of this medium has proved a stumbling block to a sound and valid appreciation of his artistic accomplishments. Generally, those who perceive him as a rock and roller are scarcely aware of his real poetic depth while those who should be aware of it often are not, mainly because a condescending attitude toward the medium of rock and roll keeps them from looking closely enough to discover it.

In all this I am reminded of what Ralph Waldo Emerson wrote about Shakespeare, that in his own day he was merely "A popular player – nobody suspected he was the poet of the human race." Emerson also remarked that the theater in Shakespeare's day (perhaps like rock and roll today) "was cheap and of no account, like a baker's shop."

I am not suggesting that Dylan may be the unsuspected contemporary poet of the human race. I doubt that anyone is, or can be, here at the edge of history. But I do maintain that for all his fame and the considerable wealth it has brought him, Dylan remains virtually misunderstood, and in a certain ironic sense, an *unknown poet*.

Now in the new millennium, Dylan's popularity remains uncannily strong, though it is weirdly spectral compared to what it was in 1966 when the *New York Times* polled American college students with the question, Who is your favorite American poet? To the consternation of many other, more traditional poets, the overwhelming response was: Bob Dylan. Admittedly, this result had something to do with the psychic temperature of the 1960s. Perhaps the times have changed enough by now to call for a fresh perspective.

As songwriter, musician and performer, Dylan has demonstrated noteworthy talents that even hostile critics do not deny. Yet none of these designations, nor all together, quite describes what it is that Dylan does. Although his chief claim to fame is probably his genius for songwriting, his songs are not all of one kind. More or less traditional ballads such as "The Lonesome Death of Hattie Carroll" and "Hurricane" are good examples of fine songwriting that would have earned Dylan no small success. But over and above such songs as these are other kinds of songs in which Dylan reaches out in two different directions: in one toward the poem and in the other toward the psalm. Imagine a triangle with its points labeled: Poem, Psalm and Song. What Dylan achieves at his best happens in the center of that triangle. In his poetic reach he is an artist and in his psalmodic reach he is a wisdom writer. When he achieves both within the balance of *Song* he is an ecstatic spiritual lover. Thus, his best songs exhibit three aspects in search of the beautiful, the true and the good.

Naturally, poets have always felt that there is a certain mysterious and even magical quality involved in language and with the use of words. This magic, or mystery, has to do with *inspiration* and for the Christian, one would suppose, it has to do finally with the mystery of Christ as the Incarnate Word. But in this age of the computer when we live in an environment of information, the magic tends to disappear more and more from written language. As far as inspiration is concerned, the oral modes become increasingly important, and for good reason. With the speaker who is speaking or with the singer who is singing live to an audience, it becomes possible for inspiration to reveal itself in such things as the strength and timbre of the voice, in emphasis and spontaneous rhythms. Where real inspiration exists, words can take on a deeper magical resonance as a mysterious quality alive in the voice itself, which is not transferable to the printed page. In this respect, recordings are potentially a happy compromise between the printed word and the oral to the extent the artist was enlivened by inspiration at the moment of recording.

So, the first thing to take note of is Dylan's voice. There is something in the timbre of his voice, a haunting power and fullness. Listen to Dylan's early recordings now that the psychic atmosphere is so different from what it was in the 1960s, and concentrate primarily on the voice rather than on the words or the music. The amplitude of this voice, its tonal depth, has an almost elemental force. It is something of a surprise to realize that such a voice came out of a young, frail-looking wisp of a lad. The largeness of this voice, rich in matured (one could even say weathered) convictions, is an uncanny contrast to the fragile physical features of the young man out of which it came.

And then there are the words. Undoubtedly Dylan's lyrics are among the strangest to be encountered in popular music. The rich complexity and personal obscurity of the modern poet are here – only sung to folk music, folk-rock, rock and roll or whatever. But the deep meaning of the lyrics often towers above the medium in much the same way that the voice towers above the delicate frame of the youthful minstrel.

Then there is the music per se, which is as unique and innovative as anything in the popular music field. Delivered with studied expressiveness, it often goes to the brink of what most people would like to call music. There is almost always a peculiar blend of harshness and tenderness that challenges the standard notion that music should aim to be soothingly melodious. In any case, Bob Dylan's musical genius was already recognized as early as 1970 when he was awarded an honorary Doctorate of Music by Princeton University.

But the real beauty of the music cannot be fully appreciated until the riddles contained in the lyrics are understood because only then can the organic unity of music, words and performance work its special artistic magic.

2

DYLANFOLK

> Thy trivial harp will never please
> Or fill my craving ear;
> Its chords should ring as blows the breeze,
> Free, peremptory, clear.
> No jingling serenader's art,
> Nor tinkle of piano strings,
> Can make the wild blood start
> In its mystic springs.
> The kingly bard
> Must smite the chords rudely and hard,
> As with hammer or with mace;
> That they may render back
> Artful thunder, which conveys
> Secrets of the solar track,
> Sparks of the supersolar blaze.
>
> -Ralph Waldo Emerson

Bob Dylan may or may not be the poet of our time, but he is certainly the poet for what may be perceived as a kind of *folk,* which is to say, for a collection of souls responding to a common spiritual vision. The individuals that comprise this folk may not all agree on every detail of the vision, but they agree that Dylan's expression of it is of value, and they pay tribute to it by continuing to buy his albums. This core group continues to buy his albums despite the fact that those recordings get only minimal air-time on the radio and only a basic level of promotion. For the folk, a new Dylan album is an event about which they need hear only once.

In olden times a folk was a tribe, a collection of individuals bound together within a limited geographical area by customs and rituals that reflected their common spiritual perception of life. They shared this vision as if it were part of their common blood and their individual identities were inextricably tied up with being a member of that particular tribe. But today as we move toward the global village, things are different.

Individual identities are now cut loose from blood, from customs and rituals, and emerge haphazardly within an expanding cloud of turbulent ideas, grey surmises, and barely conscious attractions. Souls gravitate toward what attracts them, not through locality and blood, but through a psychic resonance with whatever touches them deeply from the far-flung reaches of time and space. As a result, myriad outwardly imperceptible tribes exist, and though they remain more or less discreet they interpenetrate each other the way countless radio signals occupy the same air, each broadcasting its own program. What unifies any one of these tribes is nothing physical. Though the individual souls are scattered in space, they come together in a shared spiritual vision.

The common spiritual perception of life at the center of any such folk-group is not a rigid, authoritarian organizing force as in the old days. It is a delicate unspeakable sense of truth around which souls become aligned *by virtue of their individual efforts to discover themselves.*

The organization of souls into tribes today is thus a much more subtle event than in earlier times. Whereas formerly one received one's identity from the folk, now one discovers oneself to be part of a particular folk only after working out one's own sense of identity. In the new folk-group individual identity is primary. It is truly a matter of birds of a feather flocking together – not physically in space, but in the spirit. It is rather like the way Swedenborg perceived the angels arranging themselves in heaven, automatically, as it were, according to the natural harmony of their innate qualities.

Nor are the tribes today clear-cut, easily discernible entities; they are fluid and cloud-like. One changes tribes as one's individual identity either deepens or dims. Although there is undoubtedly a hierarchical relationship among the tribes, it cannot be seen or known abstractly from without but can only be discovered inwardly through a process of gradual self-development. And you can't arbitrarily join "the elect," you can only become one. Nor can it be faked.

I believe Dylan speaks to and for such a tribe. Of course, to begin with, he only speaks to and for himself, and only secondarily speaks to and for the tribe as a consequence of psychic resonance. He is not the chief of the tribe, but rather a major functionary, like the skald or bard of old, whose office was *to enliven the imagination of the folk with its inner sacred truths.* A listener from any other tribe will doubtless appreciate Dylan's songs only insofar as his tribe is akin to Dylan's.

There is a magical aura surrounding Dylan, magical in that it permits one to see almost anything one wants to see. Hence, there exists a wide range of contradictory perceptions, from Dylan-the-huckster to Dylan-the-holy-man. It depends, finally, on what tribe you happen to be a part of. This book is a discussion of Dylan's songs intended primarily for a specific tribe.

The aura, which permeates both the man and his work, is rife with sleight-of-hand paradoxes, slippery ironies, and apparent ambiguities. Consider: A man became a millionaire at 21 by writing songs so personal that 40 years later many of them are still very little understood. This is a paradox to boggle the mind of any global economist or businessman. Consider: A man taking on the ancient role of singing deliverance to the captives appears in the guise of a rock and roll celebrity. This is an irony befitting our strange times. Consider: A man of conservative faith has nevertheless given that faith a decidedly radical expression. This is an ambiguity to confound the wise.

An aura is an invasion of another dimension upon the ordinary, upsetting the usual balance of things. An aura, which is more felt or sensed than seen, puts upon us a special burden. Because of the aura, we cannot perceive the object in the usual way. The only way to approach an object around which we feel such an aura is by looking inside ourselves. An accurate physical perception depends upon an honest spiritual perception. The presence of this aura brings about a kind of fail-safe situation in which one understands Dylan and his lyrics only to the extent one understands oneself.

Let us begin this discussion by looking for the thief who kindly spoke.

3

THE THIEF WHO KINDLY SPOKE

> We are hidden in ourselves,
> like a truth hidden in isolated facts.
> When we know that this One in us
> is One in all, then our truth is revealed.
>
> -Upanishad

To understand Bob Dylan's lyrics it is often necessary to listen with the ears of a child, the child you were before you were blitzed by the accumulated trash of an epoch. The mystery charged picture-language Dylan has created in his songs is a first cousin to the wisdom language that has carried fairy tales down from the lost beginnings of time to the present. It is a language, for the most part, of pictures that correspond to inner psychic events. It is not comprehensible save through imaginative feeling and rigorously honest introspection.

Dylan released the album *John Wesley Harding* in 1968 after nearly two years of public silence following his motorcycle accident. Its quiet tone, besides marking a shift in the direction of Dylan's own music, was in sharp contrast to the wild experimentation that then seemed to be going on among the big names in rock and roll. With *John Wesley Harding* it was as if Dylan signaled that he was not a part of all that. The comparatively softer and slower music of Dylan's album was soundly traditional. The lyrics, subtle and mystical, were poetic creations soaring above the fashions of the music scene.

One of the songs on this album, "All Along the Watchtower," is a particularly good song with which to begin our exploration of Dylan's work. Jimi Hendrix did a heavy-rock rendition of it, making it perhaps the best known and most widely heard song from the *John Wesley Harding* album.

This song has the advantage of being short, a mere twelve lines. More importantly, it contains an essential insight into the unmanifested dimensions of man's being, which is part and parcel of Dylan's spiritual perceptions. A clear understanding of this song will help us unravel the many riddles that are set in Dylan's lyrics like jewels in a tiara.

This song is composed in four stanzas: two quatrains followed by two couplets. The first two stanzas relate a brief dialogue; the third and fourth move on to paint a single picture viewed from a double-layered perspective. As with many of his songs, Dylan has here interwoven the obvious with the not-so obvious in an artful way that invites the active participation of the audience in order to penetrate the song's meaning.

By active participation, I mean meditation. This song is the product of an honest and inner, and even prayerful, questing for personal yet universal truth. It requires an equally sincere and honest response from the inner as well as the outer man, before it will yield up its full import. As a built-in barrier, this requirement serves as something more than a mere defense: it invites spiritual communion.

For what Dylan is offering us is an experience of intuitive insight. "All Along the Watchtower" is so constructed that a meditative listener is led artfully toward the experience of a specific intuition. When he discovers the meaning lighting up within him, he has all the proof he needs of its truth. Argumentation is then beside the point. He has become something more than he was before, both by virtue of having experienced this intuition out of himself, and by virtue of having exercised his capacity for free spiritual activity in attaining it.

Now to the song itself. It begins:

> "There must be some way out of here," said the joker to the thief
> "There's too much confusion, I can't get no relief"

This opening immediately draws our attention to the familiar exasperation we have all known and experienced whenever we have felt trapped by the circumstances of our lives. Dylan, the artist, by not stating explicitly who these two are, this "joker" and this "thief," invites his audience inward to ponder their identity. Until we identify these two, the full meaning of this song and this dialogue will necessarily remain hidden on the far side of the riddle.

The joker's lament, continuing in the next two lines, suggests the basic injustice inherent in the joker's situation:

> "Businessmen, they drink my wine, plowmen dig my earth
> None of them along the line know what any of it is worth"

While we are alive here on earth, we are all aware of the burdens put on us by the business world and by the practical demands of life, distracting us and disrupting our equilibrium. And yet, none of the agents of these forces knows what any of it is worth. In the next stanza, the thief acknowledges the validity of the joker's complaint. He then goes on to add, by way of a challenge, the cautionary reminder that they, the joker and the thief, have already moved beyond the point of taking life to be a joke. This gentle reminder is a first indication of the extremely intimate nature of this dialogue. The challenge presented by the thief intensifies and underscores the urgency of their conversation:

> "No reason to get excited," the thief he kindly spoke
> "There are many here among us who feel that life is but a joke
> But you and I, we've been through that, and this is not our fate
> So let us not talk falsely now, the hour is getting late"

Is life a joke, or isn't it? If you are no longer satisfied with the notion of life as a joke, and if you are keenly aware that time is running out, then you will feel the urgent need to *seek the truth now.* This is no time to talk falsely, especially to yourself.

If you meditate on this song, you will realize the intimate nature of this dialogue. This conversation between the joker and the thief takes place in some form within the deep recesses of every man's being, in the conscience. As merely a joker, we are prone to think that we do not really know what's going on in life and that life is somehow unfair to us. We are apt to complain and feel sorry for ourselves.

The "joker," in short, is the wild card; it can be anyone; *it is the ordinary ego experiencing itself in isolation.* The thief, on the other hand, is the darker, more mysterious side of the self. He is an "outlaw" in the Dylan sense of "to live outside the law you must be honest." It is this thief, speaking as *the still, small voice of conscience,* who speaks "kindly," robbing the ego of its cherished illusion.

The joker is the ego of illusion, unable to penetrate to the spiritual depths where unity is known. The joker, wanting to be the highest card in the deck, even if only temporarily, can not comprehend the mystery involved with the ace, that it is simultaneously the highest and the lowest card in the deck. Only when he surrenders himself to that mystery can the joker function as an "ace." The "ace" can only operate through the joker when the joker *as joker* evaporates.

The point is that there are two sides to the self for which Dylan has found intriguingly appropriate names. The joker represents that aspect of the self that is intellectually conscious of itself in its separateness from all else. The thief represents that aspect of the self that is spiritually conscious of itself within the unity of the Great All. These two, the joker and the thief, are perpetually at odds with each other.

The Joker as the ordinary worldly ego eats of the Tree of Knowledge while The Thief, hiding out in the cave of the soul, eats of the Tree of Life. The Thief is inwardly allied with "first life," with our original innocence before the disturbing influence of self-consciousness comes into play, from which the always questionable life of The Joker springs. The Thief is that side of the self that is more deeply and more vitally involved in the profound mystery of life and is not readily visible to consciousness. The voice that speaks to us out of this deeper dark side of the self is the still, small voice of the conscience, the voice of the Thief who speaks softly and "kindly."

This Thief is like a miniature version of Christ within us. Like Christ, he comes from a place beyond the letter of the law, from the spirit; and he goes beyond the evidence of the senses to the substance of things unseen. It is with this thief side of our being that we know intuitively that life is not a joke and that we had better not try to kid ourselves, because death is coming.

The dialogue recorded in the first two stanzas of "All Along the Watchtower" is thus a picture of a primary conflict that persecutes every soul struggling with the question of its reality. This conflict is no small matter to be settled intellectually after a moment's thought. It surges continually in the subterranean reaches of the soul, calling for a commitment that can only be made with the whole of our being. Dylan accurately portrays the fine balance of this inner agon when he cites a certain validity to the ego's point of view:

> Businessmen, they drink my wine, plowmen dig my earth
> None of them along the line know what any of it is worth

It is true, of course, that we are all victimized and sold short by the ways of the world. Yet, we also sell ourselves short, and others as well, until we come to realize the crucial fact that life is not a joke. Once we have heard this kindly spoken message of the Thief, we can then move on to develop this faculty as a living connection with our own deep reality, which extends far beyond anything The Joker is able to understand. Our conscience becomes, so to speak, our connection with that vast dark region that is the unknown depths of being. Hiding away in those depths is the Thief, our conscience, seeking to rob us of our illusionary and egocentric possessions, our superficial capital.

Dylan first gives us this picture of a primary conflict raging in the soul. Then in the last two stanzas, he throws light on it from two different angles, which allows us to consider it from two contrasting perspectives. In the third or penultimate stanza Dylan floods the picture of this conflict with the light from spiritual heights, while with the final stanza, he reveals the inner angst experienced by the soul down below who is as yet unaware of those heights:

> All along the watchtower, princes kept the view
> While all the women came and went, barefoot servants, too
>
> Outside in the distance a wildcat did growl
> Two riders were approaching, the wind began to howl

Here we have a key to understanding Dylan's poetic language, in which "women" and the female gender in general symbolize the soul, while the male gender symbolizes the ego. This symbology, it may be noted, has a long history in lyric poetry, reaching back at least as far as the troubadours of medieval times, as well as to the Sufi poets who were their predecessors.

The princes who keep the view are egos who have been crowned with spiritual vision, who have attained transcendental transfiguration of their being. Looking down upon the world from their ethereal and eternal vantage point, they watch human souls continually coming and going, even those without shoes, those who must meet the rude earth with their naked soles. Down below, however, the inner reality experienced by the soul whose ego has not yet been crowned is that outside, somewhere, a beast is growling, and that inside the wind (the spirit) is howling. All the while, two riders approach.

This is precisely our situation: Caught between the certain confusion that torments the uncrowned ego and the dark uncertainties of the soul, we see two riders advancing on us. To go with the ego, the Joker, is to reduce life to a joke. To go with the Thief means opening up to the unknown, which is a realm beyond the capacity of the ordinary ego. To go with the Thief requires faith. The choice is always and ever ours to make, but the moment of decision is made difficult by the ever present growling of the beast and the constant howling of the wind.

* * *

How much time do we have?

Individually, three score years and ten; seventy years on the average. Some a little more, some less. It is very little compared to the millions of years man has inhabited the earth. It is nothing within the vast stretches of time encompassing the stars. If our existence were limited to three score years and ten, we could hardly say we exist at all. Such a paltry existence would be meaningless except within the context of some larger spiritual life.

Standing here, we look to the future: death. When we consider that mysterious black hole in the future, we are naturally afraid for ourselves. Out of this fearful egotism, many become religious in the hope of immortality. But eternal life is beyond time: there before birth as well as after death (and like the blind spot in the eye, present with every passing moment). If we but turn around to examine the miracle of birth for evidence of the eternal, it becomes possible to rise above the egotistic concern for immortality, free of the fear that darkens our days. This is what Ralph Waldo Emerson did and is why he could write, "Infancy is the perpetual messiah, which comes into the arms of fallen men and pleads with them to return to paradise."

The miracle of birth and the mysterious unfolding of personality in childhood, when we view it without the restrictive limitations of contemporary science, can confirm us in a spiritual life beyond the gates of time. Although the contemplation of death may make us "religious" out of fear, the contemplation of birth can give us a sense of the eternal, which can release us from that fear. And unless we can get free of that egotistical fear, we can not experience the free spiritual atmosphere in which love becomes possible.

In early childhood, we see the soul before its fall into egohood. The child acts as though the whole world were his because, living in the afterglow of spiritual unity, he experiences the world *as himself*. Gradually he begins to differentiate himself functionally as an individual now alive in the world, on the basis of his immediate body-experience, until at last he begins to refer to himself as "I," usually at about the age of three. His memories of experiences in the world then begin to adhere to and to form themselves around this "I" to become eventually his ordinary ego, socially identified by his given name. His pre-earthly soul life, sleeping in infancy, radiates within as an unconscious after-image, which like a setting sun, recedes as the body grows. At the same time his ordinary, earthly ego rises like the moon – its cosmic symbol – into the night sky of earthbound consciousness.

And God said, "Let us make man in our image, after our likeness."

How is man the image of the Great All, in whom we live and move and have our being? Our bodies, being of the earth, are like the earth. The ego circling overhead first waxes and then wanes, going from youth to advanced age. And like the moon, this ego is no true light of itself, but a reflection of the true light, which shines from the other side – the spiritual side – of the body. The soul, being solar, abides with the spiritual sun, asleep in eternity, dreaming life.

"We are such stuff as dreams are made on," Shakespeare wrote. In the night sky of earthbound consciousness we gaze upon our moon-egos and dream our lives until we experience what mystics have called "seeing the sun at midnight." But even while we are asleep in the dream of our individual lives, we are all one in the light of the spirit, even as the light from separate candles in a dark room merge to form one light.

"The light shone in the darkness, and the darkness comprehended it not." The ordinary ego cannot comprehend the mystical fact that its life, its light, is from above unless it consults with its dark side and there hears the voice of the Thief, the conscience. The conscience, on the dark side of the self, is our soul-life in the shadow created by the ego, and our faculty, however faintly developed, for knowing in concert with the spirit above.

To "see the sun at midnight" requires, to begin with, faith. And faith, as it is written, comes by hearing. The Joker remains merely a joker till he begins to hear the Thief. Perhaps this inner dialogue has something in common with St. Paul's words to the Philippians, "For our conversation is in heaven; from whence also we look for the Savior, the Lord Jesus Christ."

4

FROM A CHROME HORSE FALLING

> Real life begins when we are alone, face to
> face with our own unknown self. What
> happens when we come together is
> determined by our inner soliloquies. The
> crucial and truly pivotal events which mark
> our way are the fruits of silence and of solitude.
>
> -Henry Miller

Many of Dylan's best songs are nothing else than poems that describe precisely those "crucial and truly pivotal events which mark our way." It is from such private, inwardly naked moments that real life begins. Indeed, it is literally in just such moments of silence and solitude that we come to see and understand most clearly that "he not busy being born/Is busy dying," as Dylan put it in his 1965 song, "It's Alright, Ma (I'm Only Bleeding)."

In "All Along The Watchtower" the business of being born is accomplished first of all by attaining the inner perception of the self as a being divided into the *Joker*, who as the moon-ego faces outwardly the illusive light of the world, and the *Thief*, who faces inwardly the light of the spirit. Having attained that inner perception, one arrives at a point of decision from whence it is possible to choose, out of a fundamental freedom, to make the leap of faith.

In the course of this book, we will explore various aspects of the *Joker* and the *Thief*, as they have come to expression in many of Dylan's songs over the years. We will come to see that out of the *Thief* side of the self a soul-faculty for perception in the spiritual world evolves, which the poet personifies with such names as "Precious Angel" and "Covenant Woman." At the same time we will come to appreciate that out of the *Joker* who refuses to hear the *Thief*, the "Dead Man" and the "Jokerman" of Dylan's later songs become the embodiment of unconscious adversarial forces.

But, to begin with, this *Joker* is, as was said earlier, the ego of illusion. In a sense he is the "son of perdition" since he is that part of our being that must die. His death will come either as one of those pivotal events while we are busy being born or it will come at physical death when the mighty power of the cosmic spirit does for us what we have failed to do for ourselves. But this failure to "die" while still alive in the body is just that which restricts and diminishes life on earth. For without this death, we remain isolated beings and like Adam, who fell from paradise, from spiritual unity, we must experience ourselves atomistically whirling through life, inherently capable of enormous explosive destructiveness.

In a sense, the death of this moon-ego, the *Joker*, is the first step toward re-entering the Gates of Eden, the beginning of a re-ascent from our inherited fallen state. This death is the great divide, which separates the twice-born from those who have not been born-again. To the twice-born, the others are living in the false light of the world, struggling blindly against their fate, unaware even how the hidden powers of the world conspire to keep them from this very death. Dylan's song, "Gates of Eden" (1965), is written from the yonder side of this death, which is why the light of this world is called "the foreign sun":

> The foreign sun, it squints upon
> A bed that is never mine
> As friends and other strangers
> From their fates try to resign
> Leaving men wholly, totally free
> To do anything they wish to do but die
> And there are no trials inside the Gates of Eden.

Political freedom, as wonderful and important as it is, does not of itself lead necessarily to real freedom. We can be free to vote or free to choose which brand to buy, but until we "die" we will not be free within ourselves, free to discover and explore our true spiritual being as creators made in the image of our Father. The lie of the world is that we are something in and of ourselves and separate from all others, and this lie is based on a blindness to the spiritual as the ground of reality. As long as we are under the spell of this lie, we remain in bondage to what appears to be the accidents of fate. After the death of the moon-ego, however, these accidents of fate begin to be seen in quite a different light, and we realize that, free in spirit, we can begin to create our own destiny. Only we cannot do so by ourselves since we are nothing in and of ourselves. With the "death" of the moon-ego, we are free to choose and are able to make the leap of faith, abiding in surrender to our own higher being, which is spiritually united within the All to the Father

Spirit. Within that unitary experience, we can wait patiently and trustingly for the response of grace, without which we create nothing.

In a sense, the original sin is that the *Joker*, the moon-ego, mistakes itself for the sun, the spiritual sun. It is the sin we are all born with because it is born with the ego, and so every man is *ipso facto* a sinner. "Sin" here is understood as "missing the mark," and so a "sinner" is one who, in mistaking the moon-ego for himself, has missed the target of truth. As long as we continue to live under the illusion of a separate ego, we necessarily contribute our share to the chaos and evil or destructive conditions of the fallen world. Thus, we have finally no one to blame but ourselves for our unhappy lot in the world.

Dylan was keenly aware of all this early in his life. On the yonder side of this death he was busy being born, busy discovering and exploring the spiritual dimension of his real being. Securely stationed in this personal faith, Dylan was able to write a little song in 1967 called "I Shall Be Released." This song is made in three eight-line stanzas, but the last four lines in each stanza are the same, and so they serve as a refrain. The laconic lines of this folksong progress by means of a logic that is not at first obvious:

> They say ev'rything can be replaced
> Yet ev'ry distance is not near
> So I remember ev'ry face
> Of ev'ry man who put me here
> I see my light come shining
> From the west unto the east.
> Any day now, any day now
> I shall be released

If the life of a man were limited to three score years and 10, if there were no greater spiritual life toward which a man advances, then indeed physical things would be the real things, and physical things can always be replaced. But for Dylan there is a life in the spirit toward which a man may advance. It is not easy, for a man must go the distance *within* himself – as Dylan has – to discover the spiritual as the real. Having gone the distance, Dylan can look back to remember every face of every man who put him here, who aided him either consciously or unconsciously to find the truth. Dylan knows that his light is from the inner sun, which he follows in the patient expectation of being released into a greater spiritual life. Any day now, but just when he does not know, *for it is not for us to know the times and the seasons which the Father has put in his own power.*

The same cryptic logic that operates in the first stanza continues in the second. It doesn't matter what "they" say, a man doesn't need protection because his only real protection is the "saving grace that's over me," and he doesn't have to fall because he's already fallen. But Dylan, at the place he has come to in his spiritual journey, is aware of his higher self beyond the boundaries of physical life:

> They say ev'ry man needs protection
> They say ev'ry man must fall
> Yet I swear I see my reflection
> Some place so high above this wall
> I see my light come shining
> From the west unto the east
> Any day now, any day now
> I shall be released

But he is surrounded on every hand by those who have not yet arrived here, by those who are still under the illusion and the lie of the moon-ego. The last stanza then presents us with the contrast between the man who has not yet known the conversion experience – or *metanoia* – and the man who has:

> Standing next to me in this lonely crowd
> Is a man who swears he's not to blame
> All day long I hear him shout so loud
> Crying out that he was framed
> I see my light come shining
> From the west unto the east
> Any day now, any day now
> I shall be released

There is a man in a crowd who is nevertheless lonely, crying out that life is unfair. This man still lives under the sign of the *Joker* and doesn't know that he, himself, is to blame. But Dylan sees *his* light come shining from the west because, having undergone the conversion experience, he's following the light of the spiritual sun, of which the outer physical sun is only symbolic, toward the greater spiritual life as he grows inwardly. But such a conversion experience is never the result of mere thinking. Rather, it is the result of intense spiritual experience like that in "All Along The Watchtower" when we come face to face with our own unknown self. Unfortunately, or perhaps fatefully, we rarely find ourselves in such a moment without being driven there out of desperation by some tragic or traumatic circumstance in life. If, when life presents us with such a circumstance, we are able to face it squarely and honestly, we will be forced to admit our utter failure and impotence as isolated beings.

And if this consciousness of failure is strong enough and thorough enough, it can shock us and jar us loose from the stubborn mind-set of the *Joker*, the moon-ego man, who is always alone no matter how many people are around him. This is why Dylan could write in "Love Minus Zero/No Limit" (1965) of his "love" (call her Wisdom, for now):

> She knows there's no success like failure
> And that failure's no success at all

Failure, real failure, means no success at all, and paradoxically, such total failure in this world can mean success in a spiritual sense if, instead of succumbing to self-pity and suicide, we face our unknown self honestly and inwardly. There is no success like such total failure when it leads to the conversion experience, without which life remains as meaningless as a rolling stone. In his song "Like a Rolling Stone" (1965), Dylan expresses in some detail what can occur inwardly as a metanoiac experience to which one is brought by an intense sense of failure. The first stanza of this now famous, but little understood, song expresses the consciousness of failure and the sense of defeat from which the conversion experience begins:

> Once upon a time you dressed so fine
> You threw the bums a dime in your prime, didn't you?
> People'd call, say, "Beware doll, you're bound to fall"
> You thought they were all kiddin' you
> You used to laugh about
> Everybody that was hangin' out
> Now you don't talk so loud
> Now you don't seem so proud
> About having to be scrounging for your next meal

This song, too, is an inner dialogue. The deep inner voice of the *Thief* addresses the *Joker*, reminding him of how he used to go blithely through life laughing at those who were down and out. But now the self has been humbled by some unspecified but sorrowful circumstance. In this song the tragedy itself is not important, but *the changes the self undergoes* are. At the brink of despair, the still, small voice of the *Thief* speaks kindly even if tauntingly, pushing us to face our situation squarely:

> How does it feel
> How does it feel
> To be without a home
> Like a complete unknown
> Like a rolling stone?

In the next stanza we meet Miss Lonely, who is lonely like the man in the crowd of "I Shall Be Released." She is a personification of the awareness or consciousness of the one undergoing this metanoiac experience. She has learned a lot in the school of life, but so far she has only gotten juice instead of meat, instead of that which could truly sustain the soul. She's never learned what it means to be out on the street, out in the cruel world really on her own. But now she will have to find a way to get used to it. But how? In the past she's never wanted to have any dealings with the "mystery tramp," that *mystery* that keeps hanging around on the outskirts of consciousness, that mystery that no one seems to take seriously or care about, that mystery that always seems to want *her* to *give up* something. But, at last, she comes face to face with this mystery, staring into the vacuum of its eyes. Staring hard into the unyielding demand of this "mystery tramp," Miss Lonely comes to realize that on the far side of despair there is no excuse or alibi for *not* giving up:

> You've gone to the finest school all right, Miss Lonely
> But you know you only used to get juiced in it
> And nobody has ever taught you how to live on the street
> And now you find out you're gonna have to get used to it
> You said you'd never compromise
> With the mystery tramp, but now you realize
> He's not selling any alibis
> As you stare into the vacuum of his eyes
> And ask him do you want to make a deal?

The unyielding demand of the "mystery tramp" remains always, of necessity, an unspoken demand because it issues from the very dark, and one might say, pre-verbal depth of our being into which the realization of failure has plunged us. Indeed, the demand is to give up the illusion of the moon-ego, the *Joker*, and to turn to the spirit. Asking the "mystery tramp" to make a deal is tantamount to praying to the spirit for help. In the depths of despair, and up against the wall beyond which the mind cannot go, this prayer is not so much voiced in words as in the whole straining and yearning of our being. Listen to the way Dylan expresses these lines in his recording, and you will get an idea of how his vocal articulations can often be taken as a kind of poetry beyond words.

It is in the next stanza, the third stanza, that the actual conversion happens. There is an inward "turning around" of this consciousness, of Miss Lonely, as she experiences a rapid series of disillusionments, not the least of which is that she has always allowed other people to get her "kicks" for her. Interestingly enough, this word, "kicks," includes both the joys and the hard knocks of life. Books, magazines, TV, movies, etc., surround us with a flood of *vicarious* experience. But in this song, Miss Lonely must undergo a real-life experience by accepting her failure and going through it to find the rock-bottom self up against the mystery of existence. The still, small voice of the *Thief* guides her through:

> You never turned around to see the frowns on the jugglers and the clowns
> When they all come down and did tricks for you
> You never understood that it ain't no good
> You shouldn't let other people get your kicks for you
> You used to ride on the chrome horse with your diplomat
> Who carried on his shoulder a Siamese cat
> Ain't it hard when you discover that
> He really wasn't where it's at
> After he took from you everything he could steal

The climax disillusionment, so to speak, is expressed in the images of the last five lines. To realize that before this tragic experience of failure plunged you into despair you had been gaily prancing through life on "the chrome horse" is to realize that you had been riding high on the illusion of the moon-ego. And when you were up on that *high horse*, full of pride, you carried on your shoulders a Siamese cat, which is to say, the intellect by which it is possible to reason now this way and now that, in order to justify yourself and maintain the polish on the chrome. The metanoiac experience is the realization by inner illumination that this chrome horse, and the *Joker* who rides upon it, is not really "where it's at." This is a hard discovery to make because you are suddenly overwhelmed by a blinding picture of how wrong you have been and of all that has been lost while living under that grand illusion.

This conversion experience, this falling from "the chrome horse," is perhaps not unlike Saul falling from his horse on the way to Damascus. After such an experience, one is fundamentally a different person. If before, as a *Joker*, one found Christ and the language of Christianity amusing, now in the depths of this experience one can clearly hear the call of the *world conqueror who was born in a stable*, Napoleon in rags:

> Princess on the steeple and all the pretty people
> They're drinkin', thinkin' that they got it made
> Exchanging all kinds of precious gifts and things
> But you'd better lift your diamond ring, you'd better pawn it babe
> You used to be so amused
> At Napoleon in rags and the language that he used
> Go to him now, he calls you, you can't refuse
> When you got nothing, you got nothing to lose
> You're invisible now, you got no secrets to conceal

At the peak of this conversion experience, when the illusory moon-ego is stripped away, you realize that you have nothing and that the real you, the one that is, is invisible. After this experience, you can no longer hide things from yourself under the illusion of the *Joker*, and now you know that you can no longer refuse to go to Him, to Christ, Napoleon in rags.

In this interior dialogue, the still, small voice of the *Thief* has been speaking to Miss Lonely, to the ordinary self-consciousness, the *Joker* side of the self. From a sense of total failure, Miss Lonely confronted the "mystery tramp" and staring into the vacuum of his eyes, came through to an illumination of the illusory ego on its "chrome horse." All through this experience, the refrain provokes and stings the soul with:

> How does it feel
> How does it feel
> To be on your own
> With no direction home
> Like a complete unknown
> Like a rolling stone?

Anyone who has been driven to those depths knows how it feels to be on your own, with no direction home, like a complete unknown. But only "like" a complete unknown, for when Napoleon in rags calls to us, and we go to Him, we are not unknown: *I am the good shepherd, and know my sheep, and am known of mine.*

The refrain of this song digs at the soul with its question, calling us to turn around from the lie of the moon-ego and from the mistaken belief that we are separate and something in and of ourselves. This refrain is not unlike these words from the Bible:

> What? know ye not that your body is the temple
> of the Holy Ghost which is in you, which ye have of God,
> and ye are not your own?

5

THE EXPLOSION THE NIGHT WATCHMAN SAW

> We may know little or we may know much, but the farther we push the more the horizon recedes. We are enveloped in a sea of forces which seems to defy our puny intelligence. Until we accept the fact that *life itself is founded on myster*y we shall learn nothing. (emphasis added)
>
> -Henry Miller

"He that writes to himself writes to an eternal public," wrote Emerson. "The deeper he dives into his privatest, secretest presentiment, to his wonder, he finds this is the most acceptable, most public and universally true." Dylan has often said simply enough that his songs are "just me talking to myself." Because his songs are such private, soul-searching and soul-revealing creations, they speak magically to an eternal public. The basis of this magic is the underlying spiritual unity of mankind. As

Emerson put it, "It is one light which beams out of a thousand stars. It is one soul which animates all men."

Although Emerson eventually came to call this one soul that animates all men the Oversoul, it has been known by various names. For instance, a Christian mystic might call it the Mystical Body of Christ. But naming it is perhaps not so important as recognizing it and understanding our relationship to it as an aspect of the mystery upon which life itself is founded. In his essay "Self-Reliance," Emerson indicated a very important aspect of our relationship to that mystery:

> We lie in the lap of immense intelligence which makes us receivers of its truth and organs of its activity. When we discern justice, when we discern truth, we do nothing of ourselves, but allow a passage of its beams... Its presence or its absence is all we can affirm. Every man discriminates between the voluntary acts of his mind and his involuntary perceptions, and knows that to his involuntary perceptions a perfect faith is due. He may err in the expression of them, but he knows that these things are so, like day and night, not to be disputed.

This immense intelligence, operating within that "sea of forces," which seems to defy our puny intelligence, sends its beams into us through the conscience. The still, small voice of the *Thief*, speaking to Miss Lonely, reveals a true picture of the moon-ego, which comes as involuntary perception. Whenever a perception of truth, beauty or goodness lights up in our consciousness, we may indeed affirm its presence. In the "Hard Rain" confusions of our modern times, however, it has become increasingly difficult to recognize this subtle relationship or to discover its process. Inundated with distractions, one can hardly find the silence and solitude needed to distinguish the involuntary perceptions from the voluntary acts of the mind.

Dylan's "Visions of Johanna" is about the discovery of the fact that life itself is founded on mystery and about our relationship to this immense intelligence within that mystery. "Visions of Johanna" is extremely difficult to comprehend because it is literally crammed with the imagery of that personal mystery-language that Dylan has created to explore the inner workings of the psyche. Yet, once the riddles are unlocked, it becomes possible to appreciate every word and to share in the spiritual experience the song records.

As an inner soliloquy, this song moves by stages from a deep sense of existential angst or despair to a mystical illumination. In "Like a Rolling Stone," the actual event that plunged the self into the depths was not the important thing, but rather the changes the self undergoes in those depths. It is the same with "Visions of Johanna." The biographical events, which have led the self to the experience of existential angst, have been portrayed often enough by novelists and poets of the past, and by now they are familiar features of contemporary life. In "Visions of Johanna" the story, so to speak, is the story of the subtle changes that the self undergoes as it struggles inwardly and honestly with despair.

The one undergoing this experience is called "the night watchman." He is the center-point of consciousness, the ego-being frozen, as it were, in a state of suspended contemplation. Although he is not mentioned by name until the second stanza, the details of his suspended contemplation, his despair, are rendered poetically in the first stanza. He is burdened by an acute awareness of the emptiness of life, but he is unable to rest quietly in his dark night of the soul because certain mystical ideas or conceptions, i.e. the visions of Johanna, continually return to stir things up within him. He wrestles with it all and by the end of the first stanza, he is forced to admit that the visions have "conquered" his mind, which is to say, he is unable to dismiss them if he is to be honest with himself.

> Ain't it just like the night to play tricks when you're tryin' to be so quiet?
> We sit here stranded, though we're all doin' our best to deny it.
> And Louise holds a hand full of rain, temptin' you to defy it.
> Lights flicker from the opposite loft
> In this room the heat pipes just cough
> The country music station plays soft
> But there's nothing, really nothing to turn off
> Just Louise and her lover so entwined
> And these visions of Johanna that conquer my mind

Just as in "All Along the Watchtower," the identities of the *Joker* and the *Thief* presented a riddle, so in this song do the identities of Johanna and Louise. After living with this song, meditating on it, one can come to recognize Johanna as a designation for *spiritual intuition* while Louise is a personification of Life itself. The "night watchman" is sitting in the dark pondering and wrestling with his despair. He perceives that we are all stranded and doing our best to deny it. And that Louise, Life itself, presents each of us with a handful of rain, i.e. with our individual share of pain and confusion, challenging us to defy it, to overcome it. He is aware that even though lights of hope or insight may seem to be flickering in some one else's head, in some "opposite loft," yet when he looks within himself he finds a different story. Within his own darkened consciousness he is aware only of the "heat pipes," the sputtering life-functions of the body; of the soft, country music-like sway of old emotions; and of the confounding realization that there is nothing, really nothing to turn off by committing suicide. At this naked moment of despair, he is poignantly and intensely aware of the endless entwining of "Louise and her lover," of Life and Death, and of those visions which he has been unable to discredit or dislodge from his mind.

But what are these visions of Johanna? I take them to be spiritual or mystical conceptions such as, "In the beginning was the Word...," with which the Gospel of St. John begins. In other words, they are such conceptions that cannot be clarified or defined by ordinary intellection but which point to an understanding that takes into account the fact that life itself is founded on mystery. Because such conceptions cannot be dealt with handily by the intellect, they lure us into deeper regions, and because they can ring the bell of truth deep within us, they are not easily evicted from consciousness.

As this song progresses, the relationship of the soul to these visions goes through subtle changes. At first it is just a matter of not being able to reject them, i.e. they conquer the mind. But finally, by the end of the song, after inwardly pondering the complexities of despair, the soul yields itself to the mystery when the visions become all that remain. But between these two points, the profusion of dense imagery, though making the song difficult to understand, allows the poet to express an incredible amount of inner experience in a very brief space.

> In the empty lot where the ladies play blind-
> man's bluff with the key chain
> And the all-night girls they whisper of esca-
> pades out on the "D" train

> We can hear the night watchman click his flashlight
> Ask himself if it's him or them that's really insane
> Louise, she all right, she just near
> She's delicate and seems like the mirror
> But she just makes it all too concise and too clear
> That Johanna's not here
> The ghost of 'lectricity howls in the bones of her face
> Where these visions of Johanna have now taken my place

As was said before, in Dylan's mystery-language, the female gender represents aspects of soul while the male gender represents aspects of will. In this empty lot, the world of ordinary earthly life, "the ladies," which are the souls of human beings, play a spiritual game of blind-man's bluff even though they possess within themselves the key to the mystery. The all-night girls are the souls of those living in almost total spiritual darkness, and they boast in whispers about their adventures out on the "D" train, out on their road to damnation. This confused state of affairs causes the night watchman to click his flashlight, i.e. to try to see and understand what is really happening. He asks himself who is really insane, him or them?

The rest of the stanza is a meditation on Life itself. If the souls around the "night watchman" appear to be muddled and lost, he perceives that Life itself, Louise, in and of itself, is all right except that it is so near, so involved in his own being, that it is hard to grasp. She, Louise, Life, is a delicate thing, and when you try to look at her, to meditate on Life, she or it "seems like the mirror." This is an intimation of the metaphysical perception of the outside world as an unconscious projection of one's own inner being, of the idea that we are what we see. In any case, when the night watchman thinks about Life, about Louise, she makes it all too clear that Johanna, true spiritual understanding, is not here in this "empty lot" of the world. Then the night watchman looks into the face of Life, stares into the face of Louise the way Miss Lonely stared into the vacuum of the mystery tramp's eyes, trying hard to understand. What he sees there is the bleak picture of the everyday movements of life reduced to galvanic reflex movements, devoid of meaning: the ghost of electricity.

But in this second stanza, the visions of Johanna already are working on him. They have given him the spiritual view of human souls scrabbling about in their darkness. And now, as he beholds these visions superimposed upon the bleak picture of life without meaning, he surrenders himself to them. He allows them to take his place at the center of consciousness.

By the end of the first stanza the visions of Johanna (whatever those specific insights may have been for him personally) have conquered his mind as *involuntary perceptions*. At the end of the second stanza they enliven the center of his being, and he knows that they are, like day and night, not to be disputed. Before, his thinking was merely a human thinking; now his thinking is guided by the visions. The result is that things now look different to him; they take on a new and re-evaluated aspect. To begin with, the self, which in the first stanza was thinking about suicide, is now seen anew as "little boy lost":

> Now, little boy lost, he takes himself so seriously
> He brags of his misery, he likes to live dangerously
> And when bringing her name up
> He speaks of a farewell kiss to me
> He's sure got a lotta gall to be so useless and all

> Muttering small talk at the wall while I'm in
> the hall
> How can I explain?
> Oh, it's so hard to get on
> And these visions of Johanna, they've kept me
> up past the dawn

Here, midway into this spiritual experience, the soul, under the influence of the visions of Johanna, perceives the moon-ego, who is prone to suicide, as the "little boy lost." With the greater, cosmic perspective of the visions, the ego's vanity can be seen in his taking himself so seriously and bragging about his misery. Likewise, his thoughts of suicide, of a farewell kiss with Louise, can be seen as "muttering small talk." This little boy lost is yet another manifestation of the *Joker*, but he demonstrates that the prideful "chrome horse" aspect of the moon-ego always goes hand-in-hand with the despairing little boy lost aspect. Underneath the mask of a king, a beggar's fate unfolds. This is the necessary result of the moon-ego mistaking itself for the sun.

How to explain? Indeed, how to explain this inner, ineffable transformation, which reveals the uselessness of the moon-ego? It's impossible to explain. The immense complexity and depth of what happens in this song are beyond words. One has the feeling that with this song Dylan has exploded the song-form, vastly expanding its possibilities, in his effort to express the profound complexity of his experience. That he succeeded at all is truly amazing.

In the next stanza, the attention moves from the self back out to the world, which is evaluated anew as well. In the light of the eternal, that is to say the spiritual, the idea of infinity goes up on trial. For, if there is infinity, but nothing that is eternal, then salvation begins to look like a dead and dusty museum piece. Mona Lisa, which is to say, the world of art, has become world-weary and decadent; you can tell by its frivolous and whimsical attitude, its droll smile. With religion and art both in such sad shape, the "night watchman" looks around him and can see how "the primitive wallflower," which is to say, the naive and unsophisticated soul, is easily frightened out of the dance of life whenever the bolder and artificial "jelly-faced women" do so much as even sneeze. And the macho souls, "the ones with the mustache," have no humility at all: they cannot find their knees. All this and more Dylan expresses in the following stanza:

> Inside the museums, infinity goes up on trial
> Voices echo this is what salvation must be like
> after a while
> But Mona Lisa musta had the highway blues
> You can tell by the way she smiles
> See the primitive wallflower freeze
> When the jelly-faced women all sneeze
> Hear the one with the mustache say, "Jeeze
> I can't find my knees"
> Oh, jewels and binoculars hang from the head
> of the mule
> But these visions of Johanna, they make it all
> seem so cruel

Oh, the rewards: precious spiritual treasures and clear, distant vision. These go to the one who can carry his load and hold on stubbornly until the night has turned to dawn. Still, it all seems so cruel, especially in the light of the visions of Johanna.

It still seems cruel because the transformation is not yet complete. The final surrender to the visions culminates in the last stanza, amid a crowded cast of characters:

> The peddler now speaks to the countess who's
> pretending to care for him
> Sayin', "Name me someone that's not a parasite
> and I'll go out and say a prayer for him"
> But like Louise always says
> "Ya can't look at much, can ya man?"
> As she, herself, prepares for him
> And Madonna, she still has not showed
> We see this empty cage now corrode
> Where her cape of the stage once had flowed
> The fiddler, he now steps to the road
> He writes ev'rything's been returned which was
> owed
> On the back of the fish truck that loads
> While my conscience explodes
> The harmonicas play the skeleton keys and the
> rain
> And these visions of Johanna are now all that
> remain

The peddler, as an aspect of the will within the self, is interested in selling his goods in the marketplace of the world. The countess he speaks to, who is pretending to care for him, is the soul of commerce. He says to her "Name me someone that's not a parasite and I'll go out and say a prayer for him." This is a *rationale* to justify the self's activity in the marketplace and on the surface looks sound enough. In this world it's true, we *are,* all of us, parasites, living off one another. However, the song moves into a deeper perception with this:

> But like Louise always says
> "Ya can't look at much, can ya man?"
> As she, herself, prepares for him.

No, man cannot look at much, especially when limited to his ego, and so Louise, Life, is always surprising him. The peddler has forgotten about Christ, the one exception to the parasite rule. He is aware that Madonna, the mother of the spirit, is not yet present, and he is aware also that the "empty cage," the physical body, where once her presence was felt, continues to deteriorate before his eyes. It is significant that the cage is empty because it means that the ghost that is the moon-ego has fled at this intense moment of surrender and transformation.

The fiddler is another aspect of the will. Interestingly enough, this word brings together two conceptions: the music-maker and thus the spiritually integrative part of the self, and the part of the self that has, at least until now, been content to merely fiddle with life. This fiddler now steps to the road or comes to the fore, and he settles all the accounts on the back of the "fish truck," the Christian way, while it loads, while it gathers up its flock. As this is happening, the conscience explodes. Later, in 1978, in the song, "Where Are You Tonight? (Journey Through Dark Heat)," Dylan would write, "The truth was obscure, too profound and too pure/To live it you have to explode."

The visions of Johanna are now all that remain and it is understood, finally, that the "harmonicas" – the harmony, or music of the spheres, which is to say, the cosmic spiritual powers – control not only the mysteries of life and death, but also the rain, the "Hard Rain," the apparent chaos of the world. The "harmonicas" is Dylan's name for what Emerson called "immense intelligence" and what Henry Miller called the "sea of forces" enveloping our puny intelligence. By going into and through his despair, the night watchman has been led by "Louise," by Life itself, to experience a mystical illumination of a Christian mystery.

When the "fiddler" writes "ev'rything's been returned which was owed," it reminds one of a similar expression in Goethe's *Fairy Tale of the Green Snake and the Beautiful Lily.* Goethe's fairy tale, like Dylan's song, is a story of inner transformation. And like Dylan's song, it is full of symbolic characters representing aspects of the self, and thus open to various interpretations. But at the climax of Goethe's tale, "the old man of the Lamp" says: "go and do as I advise thee; all debts are now paid."

Once the accounts are settled, the conscience, our faculty for knowing in concert with the spirit above, explodes or opens up with a blinding illumination of the all-encompassing power of the spirit.

6

COME IN, SHE SAID

> Self-centredness is the main consequence of original sin.
> Man is shut up within himself and sees everything from his
> own point of view and in relation to himself ... Self-centredness
> distorts all the perspectives of life ... we must climb out of the pit
> of self-centredness and rise to a height.
>
> -Nicolas Berdyaev

About 1967 Dylan wrote a song called "Long-Distance Operator." It was experimental and though not originally intended for release, it finally came out in 1975 on *The Basement Tapes* album, a collection of songs recorded with The Band, not at a studio, but in The Band's basement on a home recorder. It was eventually released because of extensive bootlegging. In "I Shall Be Released" Dylan sang, "Yet every distance is not near." The distance he is referring to is the distance one travels in spiritual self-transformation. The "Long-Distance Operator" is a spiritual force or power that can connect him to his own higher self, his own spiritual-soul.

> Long-distance operator
> Place this call, it's not for fun
> Long-distance operator
> Please, place this call, you know it's not for fun
> I gotta get a message to my baby
> You know, she's not just anyone

By now it should be obvious that Dylan was deeply concerned with spiritual development and inner transformation from the beginning of his career. The belief that the answers are "blowin' in the wind," which is to say, in the spirit, was no idle belief for Bob Dylan. He had experienced metanoia, or conversion, very early in life and was committed, as "Visions of Johanna" shows, to spiritual self-transformation. The "long-distance operator," as a power of the spirit, knows that the connection Dylan desires is "not for fun" and that his "baby" is "not just anyone." The understatement of the lines in "Long-Distance Operator" is so stark and bare that it borders on the flippant, which may be why Dylan was originally against releasing this song. However, the last stanza does point out plainly the problem that Dylan faces:

> Ev'rybody wants to be my friend
> But nobody wants to get higher
> Ev'rybody wants to be my friend
> But nobody wants to get higher
> Long-distance operator
> I believe I'm stranglin' on this telephone wire

Dylan is intent on spiritual transformation even if it appears to him that no one else is. This difficult task, which he has set for himself, is full of pitfalls and booby traps. Many of Dylan's songs record the ups and downs involved in untangling the "telephone wires" and in getting through to his "baby."

One such song is "I Want You" from 1966. It expresses the same longing for the revelations of the spirit found in "Long-Distance Operator," but is a more eloquent and complicated lyric. Twelve years later, he would make another recording of "I Want You" on the *Budokan* album which, by its new musical arrangement and accompanying vocals, highlighted its sacred, hymn-like quality. This song expresses Dylan's steadfast determination and also hints at the direction and nature of his spiritual path. It is a heart-felt prayer for the spiritual enlightenment of the soul that the poet, in spite of all that would keep him from it, feels is somehow his birthright:

> The guilty undertaker sighs
> The lonesome organ grinder cries
> The silver saxophones say I should refuse you
> The cracked bells and washed-out horns
> Blow into my face with scorn
> But it's not that way
> I wasn't born to lose you
> I want you, I want you
> I want you so bad
> Honey, I want you

The honey he yearns for is manna, the gift of the spirit in the form of spiritual enlightenment, or in another sense, the Honey who is his own spiritual-soul. This spiritual-soul is the other half of what he is, the missing piece. As the object of his love, so to speak, she remains in the spiritual sun, at a distance that, metaphysically speaking, is not near.

The "guilty undertaker" is a personification of the *Joker* attitude that life is nothing but a joke. If life is a joke, then one's death is meaningless, too, and the best that such a guilty undertaker can offer is a sigh. The "lonesome organ grinder" is also another manifestation of the *Joker* side of being. He is lonesome like the man in a lonely crowd of "I Shall Be Released," and like Miss Lonely in "Like A Rolling Stone." He is an organ grinder because of his obsessive self-centredness. The "silver saxophones" are the sad strains, the emotional "blues," endemic to the life of the moon-ego. But all these *Joker* forces notwithstanding, the poet *knows* within himself that he was not born to lose her. His prayer is the deep yearning for reunion with his higher being, the desire to be made whole again:

> The drunken politician leaps
> Upon the street where mothers weep
> And the saviors who are fast asleep
> They wait for you
> And I wait for them to interrupt
> Me drinkin' from my broken cup
> And ask me to
> Open up the gate for you.
> I want you, I want you
> I want you so bad
> Honey, I want you

The "drunken politician" is not someone who happens to hold a political office. He is yet another incarnation of the *Joker*, who rides a "chrome horse" and carries "on his shoulders a Siamese cat" – his personal ego-centric diplomat. He "leaps" upon the street, the world of ordinary life, the fallen world, because this is where he dominates, or would like to dominate. It is the dog-eat-dog world where the law of the jungle rules and where the mothers (mother night, mother earth, mother Mary, and "the mothers" in the Goethean sense) weep over man's spiritual ignorance and impoverishment, over man's inhumanity to man. The "saviors," the avatars, who once could teach man how to reach the spiritual world, now seem to be sleeping. They are waiting for the return of the Spirit, for an end to the "twilight of the Gods," for the end of the *kali yuga*, or dark age. And, the poet is waiting for them to return to help him open the gates for "Her."

The next stanza is different in form from the other four that make up this song. It divides the song in half. The first two stanzas express primarily his yearning. The last two express the inner actions he has taken to win his "love." But this short, four-line stanza between them indicates his determination:

> Now all my fathers, they've gone down
> True love they've been without it
> But all their daughters put me down
> 'Cause I don't think about it

Even if all his predecessors, poets and mystical lovers have been without "true love," and so failed to attain the spiritual union, he won't think about it. Fools rush in where angels fear to tread, and he will try even if the "daughters," those souls around him who have also been influenced by the same forerunners, put him down for it.

> Well, I return to the Queen of Spades
> And talk with my chambermaid
> She knows that I'm not afraid
> To look at her
> She is good to me
> And there's nothing she doesn't see
> She knows where I'd like to be

> But it doesn't matter
> I want you, I want you
> I want you so bad
> Honey, I want you

Our conscience, on the dark side of the self, is our soul-life in the shadow created by the ego, and our faculty, however faintly developed, for knowing in concert with the spirit above. Hidden within this dark side of our being, deeper even than the *Thief*, who is the voice of the conscience, is our higher spiritual self, our spiritual-soul. She resides safely within the realm of the sun in spiritual unison with Sophia, the Soul of the World. The "Queen of Spades" to whom the poet turns in his sacred yearning is Sophia, the Queen of Heaven and the Queen of Night. His returning to Sophia is an act of surrender, an inward gesture that says, "I am under your guidance."

In this inward posture of worship, he talks to his "chambermaid," which is to say to his spiritual-soul. She knows that he is not afraid to look at her, that he is not afraid to come face to face with his own unknown self in the dark mysteries of the soul. He knows that she has been good to him and that, united to the soul of the world, "there is nothing she doesn't see," however blind he may be in his limited ego-existence. She knows where he'd like to be, she knows what he is yearning for. But what he wants is not what matters. She sees and knows all, and so she knows what is best.

The last stanza of this song is the conversation with his soul, with his "chambermaid," in which he makes note of the steps he has taken toward the accomplishment of his goal.

> Now, your dancing child with his Chinese suit
> He spoke to me, I took his flute

> No, I wasn't very cute to him
> Was I?
> But I did it, though, because he lied
> Because he took you for a ride
> And because time was on his side
> And because I...
> I want you, I want you
> I want you so bad
> Honey, I want you

In this conversation with his "chambermaid" he recognizes the "dancing child with his Chinese suit" as another projection of the *Joker*, the moon-ego. As yet spiritually immature, this childish stance of donning clothes that are exotically foreign and colorful merely to impress or show-off needed to be silenced, if the self is to breakthrough to reality. In the exploding moments of spiritual transformation such as are recorded in "Like a Rolling Stone" or in "The Visions of Johanna," Dylan has taken the child's flute away, has removed his power of influence. He did it because this child lied, and because "he took you for a ride" on a "chrome horse," and because time – the fallen world of time – was on his side. At the end of this stanza where he says, "And because I ...," those three periods indicate the subtle shift of attention from the "Chambermaid" back to the "Queen of Spades." Having finished his conversation with his soul, he gazes back into the dark, spiritual distance at Sophia and resumes his prayer.

About seven years later Dylan wrote an exquisitely beautiful song called "Shelter from the Storm." We will review only a few of its 10 stanzas in order to show its intricate relation to "I Want You." The first stanza of "Shelter from the Storm" recalls that earlier period of longing for spiritual transformation expressed in "I Want You":

> 'Twas in another lifetime, one of toil and blood
> When blackness was a virtue and the road was full of mud
> I came in from the wilderness, a creature void of form
> "Come in," she said, "I'll give you shelter from the storm."

The kingdom of heaven is within, and when Dylan came in from the wilderness, when he returned to the "Queen of Spades," she answered his supplication with the promise: come in, and I will give you shelter from the storm, from the "Hard Rain" that surrounds you. There are a number of correspondences in the lyrics of these two songs that suggests a strong affinity between them. In the earlier song there was the "guilty undertaker." In the later song there is the "one-eyed undertaker" who "blows a futile horn." In the earlier song it was the "dancing child" who "took you for a ride." In the later song it's "the preacher" who "rides a mount." But somewhere between these two songs, Dylan received in a certain sense an even greater response to his longing in the form of an inner event, a moment of mystically requited love. This moment is expressed in stanza five of "Shelter from the Storm."

> Suddenly I turned around and she was standing there
> With silver bracelets on her wrists and flowers in her hair
> She walked up to me so gracefully and took my crown of thorns

> "Come in," she said, "I'll give you shelter from the storm"

But that moment of requited love was only a moment. He has gained her only to lose her, and so longs for her again. The next stanza, stanza six, reports this renewed longing:

> Now there's a wall between us, somethin' there's been lost
> I took too much for granted, got my signals crossed
> Just to think that it all began on a long-forgotten morn
> "Come in," she said, "I'll give you shelter from the storm"

In his essay, "The Over-Soul," Emerson wrote, "there is a difference between one and another hour of life in their authority and subsequent effect. *Our faith comes in moments; our vice is habitual.* Yet there is a depth in those brief moments which constrains us to ascribe more reality to them than to all other experience." (Emphasis added). The inner event of requited love is such a moment. When such a moment passes, unless we are saints or sages, we slip back into our habitual vice. Once again, we are overwhelmed by our sense of separateness and yearn with renewed passion for that mystical union, which is "true love."

As divided beings living in two worlds, we undergo this process of spiritual growth in alternations and oscillations. It is a process that strengthens our inner being the way exercise strengthens our bodies. The birth of the awakened personality is a process that takes time and involves arduous, inner struggle. The object of this process and struggle was written about by Rabindranath Tagore in his book, *Personality*:

> We have seen that consciousness of personality begins with the feeling of the separateness from all and has its culmination in the feeling of the unity of all. It is needless to say that with the consciousness of separation there must be consciousness of unity, for it cannot exist solely by itself. But the life in which the consciousness of separation takes the first place, and therefore where the personality is narrow and dim in the light of truth – this is the life of self. But the life in which the consciousness of unity is the primary and separateness the secondary factor, and therefore the personality is large and bright in truth – this is the life of soul. The whole object of man is to free his personality of self into the personality of soul, to turn his inward forces into the forward movement toward the infinite, from contraction of self in desire into the expansion of soul in love.

In "Shelter from the Storm," the poet laments his temporary estrangement from his beloved, but pledges anew his loyalty, bolstered now by the memory of his earlier rewards:

> Well, I'm livin' in a foreign country but I'm bound to cross the line
> Beauty walks on a razor's edge, someday I'll make it mine
> If I could only turn back the clock to when God and her were born

> "Come in," she said, "I'll give you shelter from
> the storm"

So ends the song. It is interesting how Dylan has made the phrase "to when God and her were born." A grammarian might think that it should read, "to when God and she were born." But unity is the condition of spiritual existence even as dividedness is the condition of physical existence. "God and her" can be understood as "God-and-her." They are eternal, outside of time, and eternally united. Dylan's phrase about turning "back the clock" is also interesting. To turn the clock back to when "God and her" were born is to turn the clock back to "existential time," to use Nicolas Berdyaev's term:

> Existential time is not susceptible of mathematical calculation, its flow depends upon intensity of experience, upon suffering and joy. It is within this time that the uplifting creative impulse takes place and in it ecstasy is known .... In existential time, which is akin to eternity, there is no distinction between the future and the past, between the end and the beginning. In it the eternal accomplishment of the mystery of the spirit takes place.

The mystery of spirit, the mystery upon which life itself is founded, is experienced in existential time, which depends upon *intensity* of experience. This intensity of experience happens in moments, usually in moments to which we are driven, as by fate, through some tragic or traumatic life-situation. But for the one who has already undergone the initial metanoiac experience and so already ascribes more reality to such moments, the painful sense of loss, of having been forsaken, which is experienced between such moments, provides the needed intensity for renewed experience in existential time. Until the process is complete, there is a continual see-sawing of ups and downs.

In the remainder of this chapter, I would like to look at two more songs that are intimately linked with each other even though there is a period of about seven years between them. Together, they can show in more detail this up-and-down of mystical striving. The first song, released in 1966, emphasizes a down phase. It is called "Just Like a Woman":

> Nobody feels any pain
> Tonight as I stand inside the rain
> Ev'rybody knows
> That Baby's got new clothes
> But lately I see her ribbons and her bows
> Have fallen from her curls.
> She takes just like a woman, yes, she does
> She makes love just like a woman, yes, she does
> And she aches just like a woman
> But she breaks just like a little girl.

Back out in the "Hard Rain" confusions of the world, he is bewildered by his soul, by his "Baby." Everybody knows that she's got new clothes, that she's been transformed, yet something is wrong. She's not so attractive now that her adornments have fallen away. She seems like a woman, but for some reason she breaks down like a little girl. The "I" of the song is confused and anguished by her woman-ways, and in despair because she has let him down. Just as he returns to the "Queen of Spades" in "I Want You," so he returns to her now:

> Queen Mary, she's my friend
> Yes, I believe I'll go see her again

> Nobody has to guess
> That Baby can't be blessed
> Till she sees finally that she's like all the rest
> With her fog, her amphetamine and her pearls
> She takes just like a woman, yes, she does
> She makes love just like a woman, yes, she does
> And she aches just like a woman
> But she breaks just like a little girl

So, he goes to Queen Mary, Sophia, the Queen of Souls, and receives an immediate response: Baby can't be blessed as long as she thinks that she's special, something in and of herself. Here, the old business of *pride* so characteristic of the *Joker*, the moon-ego, has reasserted itself within the soul as *spiritual pride*, and proves a hindrance to spiritual advancement. The soul, by permitting the re-emergence of the moon-ego in the form of spiritual pride, blocks its own growth. The individual soul, at this stage of development anyway, remains like all the rest with her own kind of fogginess, her need of some drug-like crutch or support, and her pearls of spiritual pride. With this realization and confession of spiritual pride, the "I" of the song is finished with this version or condition of his soul with whom he can no longer fit. So, he thinks back over what has happened and how it happened, and realizes it's time to quit her:

> It was raining from the first
> And I was dying there of thirst
> So I came in here
> And your long-time curse hurts
> But what's worse
> Is this pain in here
> I can't stay in here
> Ain't it clear that —

> I just can't fit
> Yes, I believe it's time for us to quit
> When we meet again
> Introduced as friends
> Please don't let on that you knew me when
> I was hungry and it was your world.
> Ah, you fake just like a woman, yes you do
> You make love just like a woman, yes, you do
> Then you ache just like a woman
> But you break just like a little girl

The poet, hungry and dying of thirst, made the decision to "come in." But what he came into was one of the many false paths of spiritual development: spiritual pride. This version or incarnation of the soul is not the "woman" he is longing for, but merely a little girl infested with the disease of the moon-ego, and so it is time for them to quit.

"Just Like a Woman" from 1966 has an inner relationship to "You're a Big Girl Now" from 1974, as the titles themselves indicate. In "Just Like a Woman," the soul was experienced as a "woman," who because of the element of spiritual pride, "breaks just like a little girl." In the later song, the soul is experienced as a "big girl now." In this song, he comes to the realization that "she" is not under his control or command but free like the spirit itself, and free from the lower, ego-infested impulses as well. As this song begins, the poet has experienced another of those moments of faith during which the nature of their relationship is revealed to him. He begins the song by recalling their latest meeting:

> Our conversation was short and sweet
> It nearly swept me off-a my feet
> And I'm back in the rain, oh, oh

> And you are on dry land
> You made it there somehow
> You're a big girl now

Their conversation, their coming together in a spiritual harmony, was short and sweet – another brief moment of faith and illumination. Now, the poet is back in the "Hard Rain" confusions of the world. But this time, he knows that she is on "dry land," the realm of the spirit and therefore, a "big girl." And he understands now just what his position is in relation to her. It is one of total humility and deference:

> Bird on the horizon, sittin' on a fence
> He's singin' his song for me at his own expense
> And I'm just like that bird, oh, oh
> Singin' just for you
> I hope you can hear
> Hear me singin' through these tears

Just like this bird, he must sing for her at his own expense and be content with the hope that she hears him and is with him through his tears. In the next stanza he makes the pledge to change, vowing that he can undergo the necessary transformation that will allow them to reunite. They've shared too much now not to try to make it through this new period of separation. He promises to make it through and prays that she will do what she can to help him:

> Time is a jet plane, it moves too fast
> Oh, but what a shame if all we've shared can't last
> I can change, I swear, oh, oh
> See what you can do

> I can make it through
> You can make it too

There is no question of spiritual pride here as there was in "Just like a Woman." She is like the spirit that bloweth where it will. He might find her anywhere. Her freedom is the price he has to pay.

> Love is so simple, to quote a phrase
> You've known it all the time, I'm learnin' it these days
> Oh, I know where I can find you, oh, oh
> In somebody's room
> It's a price I have to pay
> You're a big girl all the way

The soul as a big girl is the soul united to Wisdom or Sophia. She will not break like a little girl, but on the other hand, he cannot "own her" either. Her revelations are hers and not his. They might come from anywhere – as involuntary perceptions. He might even find her in somebody else's room, that is, he may hear her wisdom spoken to him from someone else's mouth. But he knows that he is nothing in and of himself, and that only she, Wisdom, matters. This is the point that his love for Wisdom has brought him to, and he will not now change even though it hurts whenever they are apart:

> A change in the weather is known to be extreme
> But what's the sense of changing horses in midstream?
> I'm going out of my mind, oh, oh
> With a pain that stops and starts

> Like a corkscrew to my heart
> Ever since we've been apart

He is going out of his mind, which is what metanoia is all about. Meta-noia is literally a transcendence of the mind, the awakening of consciousness above the mind. The ups and downs of spiritual transformation with its ecstasies and lamentations are like a corkscrew to the heart. But this is the price for opening the gates, for getting higher, and for going beyond the mind with its ego-limitations.

Higher Rocks: *A Transcendental Interlude*

> Art is a *tone* of voice; it is personal and expresses the ego's relationship to the unconscious. The weakness and the greatness of art come from precisely this finiteness, this limitation. Mystics and mediums are often bad artist because they are too impersonal. Without yet having achieved the cosmic impersonality of myth, their art is all unconscious, and more dream than work of art, cliché as much as archetype. The artist has an enormous ego, and that is at once the substance of his art and the weight of his affliction....
> Afflicted as the artist may be with his ego, there is no question that his finitude is what really *matters*; the verses of a poetizing saint like Aurobindo or Yogananda cannot touch the heights of the poetry of a Milton or a Yeats.
>
> -William Irwin Thompson

Bob Dylan occupies a unique and uncanny place in the cultural life of our time. He is famous as few other artists are, as a legendary and iconic figure whose art, whose *tone of voice*, is widely felt to approach the oracular authority of a prophet. The peculiar circumstance that this voice found expression through the medium of rock and roll only accentuates the weird quality of Dylan's fame, which is at once that of a rockstar but also strangely something more. It comes near to the kind of fame and honor that were once reserved for the most exalted of literary personages, that of the poet, who was recognized as the voice of the spirit. As a result, the unusual quality of the fame accruing to Dylan remains a puzzle to many and a delight to others.

The purpose of this "transcendental interlude" is two-fold: first, to pause and recap; and then to present a picture of the important transformation that is occurring in our changing times, which is both the context for Dylan's special art and the reason for the uncanny quality of his fame. Dylan stressed long ago his awareness that the waters around us had grown and that anyone who didn't want to sink like a stone had better start swimming. In the chapters that follow, we will attempt to swim along with Dylan into those deeper waters by connecting his spirituality to its roots in mysticism, on the one hand, and by showing its resonance with the wealth of esoteric or occult literature that has entered our cultural life since the beginning of the 20th century from a variety of spiritual personalities.

The Russian Christian Existentialist philosopher, Nicolas Berdyaev (1874-1948), said in his book on Dostoievsky that "A man of genius is a high spiritual phenomenon which one must approach with a believing soul." As a man of genius Dylan is such a high spiritual phenomenon and should be approached with a believing soul, which is what we have been attempting to do. What have we come to understand so far by means of this approach?

Our close examination of Dylan's lyrics has shown us that a consistent striving for greater spiritual awareness, for getting higher, is the central thrust of his art. We have learned to see how his songs frequently take the form of internal dialogues, or self-conversations, that are studded with poetically elaborated riddles. We have also seen how by solving those riddles we are able to discover the intricate and subtle details of the inner transformations that are undergone by consciousness when it is intent on "going beyond the mind," which is what the word *metanoia* literally means.

Higher Rocks: A Transcendental Interlude

We saw, to begin with, how Dylan's perception of the dual nature of human consciousness was personified as the *Joker* and the *Thief* – respectively the outer and inner manifestations of selfhood in the human being. We were able to recognize in the *Thief* a poetic representation of the conscience that lives, and virtually hides out, in the mysterious depths of our soul-life. The precise place where the *Thief* hides out is at that point where the soul is vitally embedded in the spirit, rooted there as a part of the mystery upon which life itself is founded. The *Thief* is therefore that aspect of the self that is in touch with the living unity of spirit and with the unified life of the All.

The primary work or function of the *Thief* is to steal or take away our illusion of separateness in order to awaken us to a deeper and fuller life of spiritual communion with our fellow human beings. There is, however, a great and puzzling difficulty with the conscience. It has to operate from the pre-verbal levels of consciousness if it is to be true to life in any profound sense. For if we strive to get a handle on conscience, or try to dominate it with our conscious minds, we will be constantly confronted with the subtle temptation of "working it" for our own selfish benefit, and often in ways we are not even aware of. This is the crucial point that has to be recognized and stressed, that the conscience is a will-activity that lies deeper than the intellectual operations of the mind.

And this is precisely where "The Girl of the North Country" comes in. She is the same as "my baby" in "Long-distant Operator" who is "not just anyone." She is his "chambermaid" in "I Want You." She is the woman Dylan eventually came to recognize as a "Big Girl Now." She is the one who told him to "come in," and she would give him shelter from the storm.

Dylan's second album, which was the first to contain only songs written by him, begins with "Blowin' in the Wind," considered by many his most popular song. It was a powerfully evocative recognition that the answers come to us from the spirit. It is no accident that "Girl of the North Country" was the next song on the album. As a designation for the constant feminine presence that appears throughout Dylan's work, "Girl of the North Country" is a particularly accurate one for anyone who has come to recognize in Dylan's poetic language that the "north country" represents the realm of Spirit.

The spirit is where Truth abides, Truth, which is no respecter of persons, which remains unaffected by the adverse effects of ego-centricity. As the girl of the north country, she is the soul in its native realm of the spirit. More specifically, she is the personification of a soul-faculty that inherently transcends the inborn self-centeredness of the ordinary ego, the *Joker*. She is the soul in its virginal state, undefiled by the world, and as such she is the spiritual-soul of the self. As a soul-faculty in tune with Truth, "she" is that part of our being that is inwardly open to inspiration and capable of obtaining transcendental insights.

She is the source or agency for the reception of inspirations, yet in order for her inspired insights to enter consciousness in the form of thoughts, the will must be there to give them voice. And the *Thief* is that deep aspect of the will that operates outside the laws of mere logic and lives inwardly in alignment and harmony with the insights that she attains through inspiration. The "kindness" with which the *Thief* is able to speak derives from this subtle relationship, that her insights, which are born from above, come as inspirations and are imbued with the ineffable quality of grace, which can be felt as the manifestation of divine love.

A heart that earnestly longs for truth can hear and heed the voice of the *Thief*, the most deeply honest part of the self, when it has become conscious of her as the consummate form of Beauty. These are the intimate details of a sacred process unfolding within the inner sanctum of personal consciousness

Higher Rocks: A Transcendental Interlude

in every human being, which Dylan has incorporated into his work as an act of genius. These two conjoined and rarefied aspects of our soul-life, the conscience-as-Thief and the deep, heart-felt yearning of the self for its spiritual-soul (its one true love), are the essential elements, the double axes, or double helix, uniting Dylan's vast and continually growing body of work.

No wonder he titled his 2001 album *"Love And Theft."* At 60, Bob Dylan must have been intensely aware that life is swiftly coming to an end and many of the lyrics on *"Love And Theft"* do in fact reflect that awareness, which we have yet to consider. This could very well be his last work of art. Why not let the title reflect that "love" and "theft" in his special sense of the words are the two major and entwined motifs that have characterized his work all along and that give it unity? Why not, indeed? His creativity along those lines are demonstratively undiminished on that superb album. It may be worth pointing out here that the quotation marks fore and aft in the title are an integral part of it, suggesting that the nouns should be understood in a special sense. The fact that the title is *"Love And Theft"* instead of *"Love" And "Theft"* suggests further that the connection between these two poetic conceptions is so deeply intertwined that they are virtually inseparable.

From the start, Dylan has been intent on getting higher in the spiritual sense. He has also impressively spent his entire creative life focused on observing the inner workings of consciousness as the dynamic and dramatic interplay of self and mind. There can be little doubt that he felt and saw this inner dynamic as the most primary and deepest dimension of human life. As a man of genius, he has succeeded in expressing his creativity at that level of the "cosmic impersonality of myth" and at the same time has kept it personal as art, as the expression of the ego's relationship to the unconscious. And that is why the designation of poet as commonly and conventionally understood is not quite adequate to describe this particular artist. The special "tone of voice" that *is* Bob Dylan is the voice of mythopoeic consciousness, which has been given a new form of expression by Dylan that seems especially suited to our times.

Dylan seems to have been keenly aware that the mysterious process unfolding within his own being was something new for human consciousness, and that he was himself a forerunner or pioneer of a new and higher type of consciousness that is bound to become more widespread in the future. I say that because of a curious remark he made to reporters in Spain during a 1984 concert tour:

> I don't think I'm gonna be really understood until maybe one hundred years from now. What I've done, what I'm doing, nobody else does or has done. When I'm dead and gone maybe people will realize that, and then figure it out. I don't think anything I've done has been even mildly hinted at.

A statement like that could only have been made by an enormously inflated ego or else by someone who clearly knows what he is about and is convinced of its value. Based on my approach to Dylan in this study, it should be obvious that I take this remark as the statement of a supremely conscious artist.

Now that we have made this review of our study so far, I want to turn our attention to the cultural transformation that characterizes our changing times and that provides the backdrop for Dylan's art and our study of it. First, I will draw on insights developed by the cultural historian, William Irwin Thompson, and then I will consider ideas expressed by Ralph Waldo Emerson in 1842 as a way of gaining some historical perspective.

Higher Rocks: A Transcendental Interlude

Educated at Cornell, William Irwin Thompson subsequently held teaching positions at Cornell and M.I.T. and then later at York University in Toronto, Canada. So he was a successful and recognized academic when he eventually and famously walked out of the university in the early 1970's in order to found the Lindisfarne Association. This association was a sort of extra-curricular "think tank" made up of open-minded scholars from various fields. The researches of those scholars often went beyond the limitations imposed by the bureaucratic structure of the modern university. As a *cultural* historian, Thompson could not ignore or dismiss the wealth of esoteric literature that was having a significant influence on our culture, as mainstream academics routinely did from simple ideological preference. He was an academic who eventually found himself in the strange position of being a historian aware of a cultural transition that was larger than history.

In his book, *Passages About Earth, An Exploration of the New Planetary Culture*, Thompson considered his peculiar position.

> How much easier it would be if there were only visible events to describe rather than invisible transformations to explain, if I could tell you a story. You would think an historian would be good at that, but that's just the problem: history. How can an historian deal with something larger than history, with a transformation of culture so large that it isn't an event any more?

He then proceeds to tell us the story of an experience he had which suggests how we can understand our current situation as a transformation larger than history.

Once when I was walking along the rocky seashore of Malta, the enormity of the scale of historical measurement broke in upon me. It was low tide and the strange mustard-colored rocks were full of pools then quite distant from the sea. As I looked at the forms of life, I wondered how it must seem to swim in a pool where once one had had the sea. And then the shallows became the earth and I thought of how we were once a planet washed over by great cosmic tides, and then the tides drew back and took with it all the creatures of the deep, and we were left stranded to swim in our puddles and speak of the greatness of man.

It is a long time between tides. The Maya with their mythological calendar for measuring historical time would say that the tide went out in 3113 B .C. and will not return until midnight of Christmas Eve in the year 2011. Man has had time enough to forget about the sea and make a universe of a crevice in the rock. But now you can feel the waters lift and stir; new currents are coming in, but for those of us in the universities who cannot stand the flooding of our academic boundaries and definitions, there will be terror as the mythical future becomes confused with the mythical past. Looking at the pool at my feet, I sensed the sea at my back and climbed up to the comfort of the higher rocks.

Something has already happened, something so vast that all our social-science descriptions of man cannot add up to it. The record of civilization is over, and like a record at its end, it keeps going on with the noise of a needle stuck in its rut: the revolution of the workers, the protest of the young, the new creations of the avant-garde, the rise of new forms of sexual liberation, the appearance of new religions. This side of history is over, and on the other side is myth.

Thompson, faced with the difficulty of explaining a transformation larger than history, had to resort to the art of story-telling in order to give us a picture of our situation. His picture and Dylan's seem to resonate. We are in the midst of a Hard Rain that continues to fall, so that now there is "high water everywhere" – to use Dylan's phrase. We are beginning to "feel the waters lift and stir," and "new currents are coming in.." We are at a place where, as Dylan pointed out in "Series of Dreams," "…there's no exit in any direction/'Cept the one that you can't see with your eyes."

In the description of his dilemma, Thompson was moved to climb up to *higher rocks* as soon as he began to feel the return movement of the tide. From his higher position he could see that history as the record of civilization was over and that there was now a need to move to the other side of history, to myth, in order to gain the wider and deeper perspectives of mythical thinking. Five years later in 1978, Thompson wrote in *Darkness And Scattered Light*:

> If you are going to think about the problem of time within a civilized, literate culture, there are basically two different ways to look at it. One is through myth; the other is through history. History, by definition, is a civilized, liter-

ate record of events; it is a conscious self-image of a society projected by an elite. In a sense, history is the self-image of a culture, the ego of a culture. History is controlled through education and tradition, and is monitored, if not manipulated, by elitist institutions, whether these are temples, academies, or universities. History is the story told by the elite in power and is a way of articulating human time so that it reinforces the institutional power of the elite. One of the ways the British maintained Ireland as a colony was through the writing of history. The actual role of the Irish monks and the Irish centers of learning in maintaining knowledge in the Dark Ages was blanked out, and on that blank slate even brilliant men like David Hume wrote that there was no culture in Ireland until it was brought in by the conquering Normans in the twelfth century. So historical consciousness is closely related to power and the ego of a society. For these reasons, Voltaire said that "history is the lie commonly agreed upon," and Marx, continuing in that vein, said that "the ruling ideas are in every age the ideas of the ruling class."

When we view history not just as a record of events, but as a projection of a ruling elite whose station in societal affairs parallels that of the ego, we are entering a new dimension of historical consciousness. The waters around us have indeed grown, and the conscious historian, like the conscious poet, feels the need for a mythopoeic way of thinking. In the same book, Thompson wrote:

> Myth is the mirror-opposite of history. Myth is not the story of the ego of a civilization but the story of the soul. If you apply the terminology of C. G. Jung, you can say that myth is the story of the higher Self and that history is the story of the ego. If the ego has a limited perspective on matters and always sees things through its own passions and desires, then it is not going to be concerned with the larger perspective of the evolution of humanity or the nature of divinity. Myth, by contrast, is the larger picture. To think big is to think mythically. If you are going to ask the primordial questions – Who are we? Where do we come from? Where are we going? – then you are going to fall into mythic patterns of thinking in formulating the answers. Even in constructing a scientific narrative and articulating the known facts, the narrative will fall into a mythic pattern and archetypal structures will surface out of the unconscious.

In the same book, Thompson recounts a conversation he had with the science fiction writer, Arthur C. Clarke, who is the author of the story that was the basis for the classic film *2001: A Space Odyssey*. Clarke told Thompson that "the monolith in orbit around Jupiter in the film *2001*...was a black hole, a rent in space-time which enabled the astronaut to move into another world." Thompson then reflects, "So whether we see a black hole as menacing and demonic, a cosmic *vagina dentata*, or as transformational and positive depends on our unconscious assumptions about the nature of life and death, continuity and discontinuity, time and space. And these notions of existence are not so much the *contents* of knowledge that come to us from history and science as the *structures* of consciousness that come to us from myth." Later on in this same book, Thompson says:

> Underlying the superficial movement of historical events is the structure of myth, "the arrangement of Time." Good historians like Thucydides know that the patterns of consciousness in the writing of history derive from literature and myth. It is, therefore, not surprising that Aristotle proclaimed that poetry was superior to history, for poetry presents the universal truth of events and not merely the simple accuracy of facts. The poet thinks at a higher level, at a daimonic level of hieroglyphic thought....

And this brings me back to Dylan and his mythopoeic art. As a poet, Dylan thinks at the higher, daimonic level of hieroglyphic thought. The *Joker* and the *Thief* and "the girl of the north country" are examples of hieroglyphic thought. Hieroglyphic thought is symbolic thought that comes from the daimonic level of soul-life. At that level, the will that is infused with imagination can speak "kindly" as the *Thief*, while the *imagination* that is alive at the heart of the soul, as a commanding and compelling inner Beauty, can also speak, but only "like silence, without ideals or violence." Her speaking is a silent speaking *as the image of beauty*, and as such she acts as the *daimon* for that genius we recognize in Dylan.

So we live in a time that is undergoing a cultural transformation that is larger than history. That transformation requires, among other things, that we learn to view time through myth, the mirror-opposite of history. In order for us

Higher Rocks: A Transcendental Interlude

to find adequate answers to the ultimate questions during this transition, we will have to become as familiar with the *structures* of consciousness, as previously in "historical" times we had to become familiar with the *contents* of the knowledge derived from history and science. And since Dylan's work is concerned with revealing the structures of consciousness through his art, he can be viewed as an artist of particular importance for our time.

The necessity for the transition, which we are all going through, has its roots in a fundamental division in the human race that has plagued mankind throughout "historical times." Ralph Waldo Emerson spoke about this deep division in 1842:

> As thinkers, mankind have ever divided into two sects, Materialists and Idealists; the first class founding on experience, the second on consciousness; the first class beginning to think from the data of the senses, the second perceive that the senses are not final, and say, The senses give us representations of things, but what are the things themselves, they cannot tell. The materialist insists on facts, on history, on the force of circumstances and the animal wants of man; the idealist on the power of Thought and of Will, on inspiration, on miracle, on individual culture. These two modes of thinking are both natural, but the idealist contends that his way of thinking is in higher nature.

Though both are natural, these two distinct modes of thinking have often been the source of deep conflicts in the social life of mankind. To a surprisingly large extent, both science and religion in our day are examples of materialistic thinking, and the various putative disputes between them are essentially unwitting canards, the chief effect of which is to hide this fundamental division in mankind. The distinction made here by Emerson between the kind of thinking that takes its start from experience and the kind of thinking that takes its start from consciousness is extremely important for understanding the transition we are going through, which Thompson calls "a cultural transformation larger than history."

Human beings are innately thinkers. Indeed, the root-meaning of the word "man" is "the one who thinks." It's only natural to think about the experiences that come our way in life, and as human beings that is what we do all the time. However, to take our experiences as the primary facts upon which to base our thinking misses the central fact that consciousness is essentially the prerequisite for any experience that we *can* have.

Setting aside for the moment the idealist's contention that his mode of thinking is in higher nature, it is important to underscore that Emerson's conception of the idealist does not necessarily apply to a person who has adopted this or that ideal *as a belief*. It's always possible to believe in any given idea. However, unless that idea is more than a mere belief, it doesn't qualify the holder of it as an idealist in Emerson's sense of the term. Unless a given idea is itself founded on a thinking that has taken its start from a recognition of the primacy of consciousness over all that comes to consciousness from outside, that idea can only be held as an abstraction. The essential factor is where one begins in his thinking, either founding it on sense data and the force of circumstances or on the primacy of consciousness.

An idea held in abstraction, that is, *as a belief*, has for the believer the force of circumstance. As a belief, that idea is taken by the believer to be an indisputable fact, and he relates himself to it in the same manner that the scientist relates himself to sense data. Such a believer is not an idealist in Emerson's sense of the word, anymore than a scientist is. Both begin to think from ideas that carry for them the force of circumstance. In the case of the believer, it is a religious idea held in abstraction. For the scientist it is a non-religious idea that is equally *believed in*, namely, that sense data are the primary factors of reality. Such religious believers are, so to speak, closet scientists, as much as scientists are closet believers, and these two are secret partners on the materialist side of Emerson's great divide. This is the deeply ironic situation of modern cultural life that underlies the need for a transition to higher consciousness.

But what about the contention of the idealist that his thinking is in higher nature? How did Emerson understand that higher nature? Comparing the idealist to the materialist, Emerson says:

> He concedes all that the other affirms, admits the impressions of sense, admits their coherency, their use and beauty, and then asks the materialist for his grounds of assurance that things are as his senses represent them. But I, he says, affirm facts not affected by the illusions of sense, facts which are of the same nature as the faculty which reports them, and not liable to doubt; facts which in their first appearance to us assume a native superiority to material facts, degrading these into a language by which the first are to be spoken; facts which it only needs a retirement from the senses to discern. Every materialist will be an idealist; but an idealist can never go backward to be a materialist.

The primary facts for the idealist, on which he bases his thinking, are the power of thought and of will, which lead him to insist on inspiration and individual culture. For the idealist in

Emerson's sense of the word, these facts are superior to sense data and to the facts of history, both of which have the force of circumstance. The idealist's facts are superior because they are of the same nature as the faculty that reports them, namely consciousness. Since the power of thought and of will are prior to experience, they are able to transform material facts into a language that can be used to speak about the primary facts of consciousness. Material facts can be employed symbolically to elucidate the inner aspects of man's ideal, or existential, being, which is his real and metaphysical existence as a being of consciousness. Already in his first book, *Nature*, Emerson had written:

> Words are signs of natural facts. The use of natural history is to give us aid in supernatural history; the use of the outer creation, to give us language for beings and changes of inward creation. Every word which is used to express a moral or intellectual fact, if traced to its root, is found to be borrowed from some material appearance. *Right* means *straight*; *wrong* means *twisted*. *Spirit* primarily means *wind*; *transgression*, the crossing of a *line*; *supercilious*, the *raising of the eyebrow*. We say the *heart* to express emotion, the *head* to denote *thought*; and *thought* and *emotion* are words borrowed from sensible things, and now appropriated to spiritual nature. Most of the process by which this transformation is made, is hidden from us in the remote time when language was formed; but the same tendency may be daily observed in children. Children and savages use only nouns or names of things, which they convert into verbs, and apply to analogous mental acts.

Higher Rocks: A Transcendental Interlude

Though both kinds of thinking, that of the materialist and that of the idealist, are natural, that of the idealist is in higher nature. As Emerson says, every materialist will become an idealist, but the idealist can never go back to being a materialist. In our day, however, the materialist way of thinking has dominated our culture, both in its secular version and in its religious version, almost to the point of eliminating the idealist. The transition we are living through, which is a transition larger than history, is a culture-wide struggle to transcend the fossilized habits of materialist thinking entrenched in both historical science and traditional religious belief systems, in order to achieve the higher nature of the idealist in Emerson's sense.

As an artist, Dylan has repeatedly given strong voice to this effort. Consider these lines from the 1979 "Do Right to Me Baby (Do Unto Others)":

> Don't wanna betray nobody, don't wanna be betrayed
> Don't wanna play with nobody, don't wanna be waylaid
> Don't wanna miss nobody, don't wanna be missed
> Don't put my faith in nobody, not even a scientist

And yet his reluctance to conform to conventional religion has also been expressed, often in a slyly hidden manner, as in his 2001 "Floater (Too Much to Ask)," if we understand "the boss" to mean God and one of his "hangers-on" to mean a conventional preacher:

> One of the boss' hangers-on
> Comes to call at times you least expect

> Try to bully ya – strong-arm you – inspire you
> with fear
> It has the opposite effect

Faith has more to do with *trust* than with belief, religious or scientific, and like Emerson Dylan has pointed out that "If you want somebody you can trust, trust yourself." Otherwise, you will have to live with the paradox expressed by Dylan in his 1979 song, "When You Gonna Wake Up?" Despite having spiritual advisors and gurus to guide your every move, who promise instant inner peace, still every step you take has got to be approved. To which the only reasonable response is, When you gonna wake up?

7

THE RETURN OF THE FEMININE

> When you give up, God can give down. When you are totally
> defeated, you are totally open and receptive. Before, a spiritual ego,
> a religious self-image which was simply the ego dressed up in a
> loincloth, protected the personality and came between the individual
> and God. But in defeat and the complete humiliation of the ego,
> the individual is completely open to receive grace.
>
> -William Irwin Thompson

It is generally acknowledged that Dylan revolutionized the popular song by bringing to it the deeper concerns of social justice and moral consciousness. It is also recognized that his songs frequently focus on the individual's spiritual struggle against the powerful currents of materialism within our culture. However, what I consider to be his real poetic vocation will only be found by searching the mystery that lies at the heart of his work, namely: the mysterious female figure with whom Dylan has carried on a sort of running dialogue throughout his career in the lyrics of his songs.

This mysterious female figure in Dylan's work is like, yet not identical with, the muse, which a poet of an older time might have invoked for inspiration. If she were simply the muse in this traditional sense, Dylan would be liable to a charge of affectation. On the contrary, a close examination of the lyrics reveals a relationship often characterized by an intense tug of war between the poet and his Lady. This tug of war reflects a mystical striving within the soul of the poet not unlike that found in Sufi mystical poetry.

Robert Briffault in his book, *The Troubadours*, indicated that the *troubadours* and the vagabond *jongleurs* or traveling minstrels often took their forms and terminology from Sufi mystic poetry, which was written in an hieratic language but not accompanied by music. He then offered this interesting footnote:

> The Sufi assimilation of profane love with divine love was not entirely abstract and symbolic; the amorous experience was regarded as necessary for the comprehension of God. Love (ísk) is the union of the created with the creator.... The anguish of the lover was compared to the separation of the soul from the object of its happiness, that is to say, divine love. The "cruelty" of the beloved represented the difficulties which confront intelligence in its efforts to understand God. Thus the experience of earthly love was itself indispensable to the comprehension of the amative relation between man and God.

Did a young Dylan read this book and see in this idea of the "assimilation of profane love with divine love" endlessly fertile creative possibilities for his art? Though we have no evidence for that, it's certainly possible. It's possible, yet by no means necessary. It may only have been that a youthful Dylan, as a poetic visionary spirit of genius, experienced the dynamics of his interior life intuitively and naturally in terms of the "male" and "female" within.

In a 1978 *Rolling Stone* interview, for instance, Dylan was asked about soul mates. "What about them?" he replied. "Do they exist?" he was asked. "Sure they do," he responded, "but sometimes you never meet them. A soul mate, what do they mean by soul mate? *There's a male and a female in everyone,* don't they say that?" (Emphasis added). Later in this same interview Dylan was asked if certain lines of a song were about his being Jewish. Instead of answering the question, he gave this curious reply,

> Listen, I don't know how Jewish I am, because I've got blue eyes. My grandparents were from Russia, and going back that far, which one of those women didn't get raped by the Cossacks? So there's plenty of Russian in me, I'm sure. Otherwise, I wouldn't be the way I am.

The next question in this interview went on to another subject so that Dylan's identification with being Russian was left hanging. What could he have meant by that "Otherwise, I wouldn't be the way I am"? And why was he so at pains to make this statement? I found this seemingly gratuitous remark intriguing because I had already come to the point of interpreting the mysterious female figure in Dylan's work as a being who was for Dylan what Vladimir Soloviev's *Eternal Friend* was for him. Soloviev is not widely known in the western world, so to explain this interpretation it will be necessary to digress into a brief discussion of Soloviev and his ideas.

* * *

Vladimir Soloviev, who died in 1900, was a spiritual philosopher whose works became pivotal to the flurry of philosophical activity in early 20th century Russia that many scholars now refer to as "The Russian Renaissance." He is considered by many academics to be Russia's "greatest religious philosopher." Although his books are not widely known, his spiritual and metaphysical ideas may help us understand Dylan's lyrics better, and at the same time suggest good reasons why Dylan felt an identification with being Russian. In any case, there are clear correspondences between the mystical aspects of Dylan's art and the religious philosophy of Soloviev, who once summarized his theology in this single and amazingly succinct paragraph:

> No one has seen the Father. The Absolute is beyond perception. The Absolute is the One realized by the multiplicity of all that is. The Christ is the one who unifies the All within the Absolute. He is the only begotten of the Father, and at the same time one with Him. His active principle, which unifies the All (as multiplicity) to the Absolute (as One), is called the Logos. His passive principle, i.e. the resultant unity as a definite image of the active principle, is called Sophia.

Christ, as the supreme exemplar of the consummate individual, is composed of an active unifying principle called the Logos and a passive principle called Sophia. By reason of his Divinely active principle, the Logos, Christ unifies "the one and the many." As such, He is one with the Father and denominated "the only begotten." Sophia, as the "resultant unity as a definite image of the active principle" is the ideal and living embodiment of Divine Wisdom, and the eternal Mother of God.

In Soloviev, Sophia is perceived as the passive principle, but "passive" only in the relative sense of being that image of "the resultant unity," which lives, so to speak, in the "mind of Christ." In the Book of Proverbs, sometimes called The Book of Wisdom, Sophia is also viewed as playing a more active, though subtle, role as a living aspect of Divinity when she is called "the craftsman of God" who was there with God at the beginning of creation. As the Image of God's wisdom she exerts a powerfully subtle influence as the focus of Christ's unifying energies.

Drawing on the Biblical ideas that the human being was created "male and female" and also "in the likeness and image" of God, it would be possible to view the Logos as the archetypal Ego and Sophia as the archetypal Soul. They could be thought of as the male and the female of the divine individual, the son of God. And if it is true that we were made in that image, then we too have a male ego-principle and a female soul-principle.

This metaphysical and mystical view of the human entity, cast in terms of Christian religious philosophy, accords well with our interpretation of the mystical point of view underlying and informing Dylan's lyrics as we have so far come to know it. Dylan's mysticism can therefore be recognized as having historical and traditional roots, yet there is another aspect of our changing times that has to do with an influx of occult ideas from many different sources that has spawned an enormous amount of literature loosely referred to as "New Age."

Probably the most erudite and up-to-date source of occult ideas was the German philosopher, scientist, teacher and clairvoyant, Rudolf Steiner (1861-1925). Trained as a scientist and thoroughly knowledgeable about the fundamentals of modern science, he left a legacy of more than fifty books and more than

6,000 lectures. The last 25 years of his life were devoted to presenting and developing a worldview that was true to his own clairvoyant experience but which also recognized the actual gains to our knowledge attained by modern science. He called this worldview Anthroposophy (wisdom of man) and founded it on what he called "concrete occultism" or "spiritual science." The word occult for him simply meant that which can't be seen under ordinary circumstances, as in medicine internal bleeding is called occult bleeding. He applied the methods of modern science to the hidden and invisible, or occult, aspects of human reality, which is why his science is called a *spiritual* science.

I posit this brief paragraph on Steiner because, though he was a German who was active in the first quarter of the 20th century, he remains almost as little known in our general culture as Vladimir Soloviev. What makes him so interesting is that the modern science we know can find a place within the worldview of Anthroposophy, though Anthroposophy could never be forced into the straight-jacket of modern science. Whether or not that situation indicates that Anthroposophy represents an advance over science, as we know it, is something that each student will have to decide for himself. Despite the clarity of thought that Steiner brought to his occult ideas, his legacy has mostly been ignored by academia, yet it stands as one of the most challenging alternative worldviews to academic science.

Be all that as it may, we will make tentative use of some of Steiner's occult ideas in our further exploration of Dylan's lyrics. Our use of Steiner's ideas can only be tentative for the reason that his worldview is so all-encompassing and intricate that it is not susceptible to facile summarization. Still, if the influx of occult ideas that we have witnessed during the last century represents a new aspect of our changing times, then we may not be amiss in considering correspondences between that influx and the new kind of consciousness that Dylan has been exploring in his art.

In a book called *Cosmic Memory*, Steiner gave a description of how the essentially spiritual human entity found its way into physical embodiment at a point in cosmic evolution when the earth, as an invisible heat-sphere, condensed into a physically perceptible cosmic body in space. What is interesting here is how the essentially spiritual human entity, comprised of Will and Imagination in dynamic interplay, underlies the physical division of the sexes into the male and female forms:

> The external formation of earth resulted in that the body assumed a one-sided form. The male body has taken the form which is conditioned by the element of will; the female body on the other hand, bears the stamp of imagination. Thus it comes about that the two sexed, male-female soul inhabits a single-sexed, male or female body.

Thus, the physical division of male and female is but a reflection on the physical plane of the human spiritual entity as a creature comprised of Will and Imagination. The poles of consciousness, Will and Imagination, come to manifestation within the human as the male ego-principle whose archetype is the Logos and in the female soul-principle whose archetype is Sophia, and outwardly in the physical world in the male and female forms.

Many contemporary observers have commented on "the return of the feminine." The following may serve as a sort of crude simplified rendition of this historical perception and is offered for the sake of perspective. In the ancient hoary beginnings of human earthly evolution, a matriarchal culture ruled, which subsequently gave way to a patriarchal culture, which has dominated now for thousands of years. First the passive female principle was dominant over an infant active male principle. This would have been roughly coincident with the time in man's early history when he experienced what Steiner called "an instinctive, atavistic clairvoyance." Then, the active male principle, ego-consciousness, gradually matured and eventually began to dominate. It was necessary for the female soul-principle to give way that the ego might wax strong in order for the human individual to develop toward the possibility of freedom. But, we have now reached a critical point in this vast process where a balance is vitally needed. For if the male ego-principle continues to dominate, effectively divorced from the female soul-principle, it promises to wreak havoc upon our world. Thus, "the female" is returning but it must not be simply another flip-flop. The active and the passive, the ego and the soul, the Will and Imagination, must come together in a spiritual or conscious marriage as true partners. Just as the Logos together with Sophia make up the Christ, so must the individual wed the male and female complements of his being to become fully human.

At the mythological level of understanding it would be possible to express this spiritual process in a symbolic formulation: The Soul as the Mother gives birth to the Ego, who in turn marries the Mother when he has matured. At that stage, they attain together the image or status of the Father, who is only known through his "son," the Christ being, the divine consummated individuality.

Soloviev wrote, "As God creates the universe, as Christ builds the Church, so must man create and build his feminine complement." Actually, it is perhaps not so much a matter of building as it is a matter of remembering and re-awakening. It is, as William Irwin Thompson says in *The Time Falling Bodies*

Take To Light, that "we are lost in time and suffering from a racial amnesia," from a "loss of memory of the soul."

What we need now is for the male-principle, the ego, to rediscover its lost help-mate, the soul, and to recognize her as his spiritual complement and honor her as the way to regain the connection with his spiritual origins. When the ego in human consciousness becomes wedded to the soul in a sacred inner marriage "that no man may put asunder," that human being becomes a new man, born-again, as it were, out of his own present and personally enlightened consciousness. Out of the holy union of that mystical marriage, it then becomes possible for love-as-deed (not just as thought or good intention) to blossom. For that transformation to happen, the active and passive, the Will and the Imagination, must meet face to face in conscious harmony.

Soloviev had several visions of, or visitations with, a radiant female being whom he called his Eternal Friend, and he associated her with Sophia. Paul M. Allen, in his book, *Vladimir Soloviev: Russian Mystic*, explained that,

> ...in him had been unlocked that faculty Goethe called "the Eternal Feminine," which ever "leads man upward and on." Rudolf Steiner once pointed out that the Eternal Feminine is really a power in the human soul which permits itself to be transformed by the world of spirit and hence unites with and progresses in that world. He further indicated that this soul-faculty of the Eternal Feminine exists potentially *in every human being*, capable of lifting him into the eternal worlds.

The power by which man may ascend is a power inherent in the soul which becomes activated when the male ego-principle unites with its female soul-principle in a dynamic balance as one. Then by means of this "soul-faculty" man becomes "re-membered" to the spiritual world, undergoing – perhaps only gradually – a transformation of consciousness. When *Will* through the ego and *Imagination* through the soul come together as help-mates, then man can be born anew as a consummate human being, re-awakened to the spiritual dimension of his own reality.

It is interesting to note here that Steiner said in his lectures *The Search for the New Isis, The Divine Sophia,* that,

> The Christ will appear in spiritual form during the 20th century, not through an external happening, but inasmuch as human beings find that force which is represented by the holy Sophia.

The return of the feminine is a leitmotif that plays itself out not only on the larger stage of world culture in the form of the feminist or women's rights movements and the ecological movement, but also more profoundly within the heart of every human being regardless of physical gender. The return of the feminine within the human being, according to Steiner, is the *sine qua non* for experiencing the so-called Second Coming. When this faculty of the eternal feminine is "unlocked" the human being becomes united through its soul with Sophia. Soloviev put it this way:

> The complete realization, the transformation of an individual feminine being into a ray of the divine eternal feminine, inseparable from its

radiant source, will be the real, both the subjective and objective, reunion of the individual human being with the Deity, the reinstatement of the living and immortal image of God in man.

* * *

Many of Dylan's lyrics seem at first to defy comprehension, as if they were composed of cascading images thrown together in helter-skelter fashion. John Lennon even once accused Dylan of writing nonsense. But for those who approach Dylan with a believing soul Dylan's lyrics gradually reveal, as was said before, a sort of personal picture-language not unlike the wisdom language that has carried fairy tales down through the ages.

For instance, in 1965 Dylan produced one of the longest songs in popular recording history up to that point, "Desolation Row." More than 10 minutes long, it is composed of 10 stanzas of 12 lines each. Part of the *conceit* of the poem is that Truth in our spiritually impoverished age is condemned to live on Desolation Row. The fifth stanza is particularly relevant to the idea of the dominance of the male ego-principle in our patriarchal culture, if it be allowed that positivistic science is a manifestation of this principle, while our traditional religious forms are a relic manifestation of the old female soul-principle. In this verse, "Einstein" means science and "monk" means religion. The point is made that science has so deteriorated in our time that it is now hard to imagine that it was once a champion of truth.

> Einstein, disguised as Robin Hood
> With his memories in a trunk

> Passed this way an hour ago
> With his friend, a jealous monk
> He looked so immaculately frightful
> As he bummed a cigarette
> Then he went off sniffing drainpipes
> And reciting the alphabet
> Now you would not think to look at him
> But he was famous long ago
> For playing the electric violin On Desolation Row

Thus, the young Dylan in his early 20's painted a clear picture of the condition and position of science in his world: science "reciting the alphabet" with its interminable, arcane language investigates mainly the lower "drainpipe" aspects of reality while religion trots along shamefully behind, jealous of science's claim to authority. In these 12 lines Dylan captures the situation with richly suggestive imagery and word-play. Interestingly enough, the last two lines of the first verse of this song are,

> As Lady and I look out tonight
> From Desolation Row.

Who is this Lady that looks out with Dylan from Desolation Row? Although she appears under many different names in many different songs throughout Dylan's career, this question is most clearly answered in "Precious Angel," which is a song on the *Slow Train Coming* album, the first album in what has been pejoratively called "Dylan's born-again Christian phase." In the last stanza of this song Dylan sings,

> You're the queen of my flesh, girl; you're my woman, you're my delight

The Return Of The Feminine

> You're the lamp of my soul, girl, and you torch
> up the night

This song in which the soul is recognized as one's feminine complement begins like this:

> Precious angel, under the sun
> How was I to know you'd be the one
> To show me I was blinded, to show me I was gone
> How weak was the foundation I was standing upon?
>
> Now there's spiritual warfare and flesh and blood breaking down
> Ya either got faith or ya got unbelief and there ain't no neutral ground
> The enemy is subtle. Howbeit we are so deceived
> When the truth's in our hearts and we still don't believe?

This song, perhaps more than any other, exemplifies the inner dynamics operating between the male-ego and the female-soul principles. The chorus is a kind of chant in which the ego openly confesses his blindness without the help of his feminine complement,

> Shine your light, shine your light on me
> Shine your light, shine your light on me
> Shine your light, shine your light on me
> Ya know I just can't make it by myself
> I'm a little too blind to see

In the rest of the lyric, however, it is as if the active male ego-principle and the passive female soul-principle are face to face. Although it is the ego doing the speaking (Will), what is spoken is that which is seen or known within and by means of the soul (Imagination). That which abides within the "passivity" of the soul is revealed through the activity of the ego in the speaking:

> My so-called friends have fallen under a spell
> They look me squarely in the eye and they say,
> "Well, all is well"
> Can they imagine the darkness that will fall
> from on high
> When men will beg God to kill them and they
> won't be able to die?
>
> Sister, lemme tell you about a vision that I saw
> You were drawing water for your husband, you
> were suffering under the law
> You were telling him about Buddha, you were
> telling him about Mohammed in one breath
> You never mentioned one time the Man who
> came and died a criminal's death

These lines connect importantly with the climactic last two lines of the last stanza,

> But there's violence in the eyes, girl, so let us
> not be enticed
> On the way out of Egypt, through Ethiopia, to
> the judgment hall of Christ

This song, which has three verses each followed by the chorus, is an expression of an event in the interior life of the poet. The event is a change of perspective, a deepening of the poet's spiritual perception. The "Sister" is the soul of one of his "so-called friends" and the ego of that sister-soul is referred to as her "husband." In the vision that the poet has seen, which he would like to communicate to that Sister, he sees how this sister has been bringing the spiritual lights of Buddha and Mohammed to her husband, but without ever mentioning the spiritual light that is Christ, who is central for the poet and his own spiritual-soul, his "precious angel." We live in a time of spiritual warfare when flesh and blood are breaking down, and in the spiritual depths the poet knows that on the way out of Egypt, the land of bondage, to "the judgment hall of Christ," they cannot be swayed by that particular point of view held by his "so-called friends," because:

> Precious angel, you believe me when I say
> What God has given to us no man can take away

"Precious Angel" is on the *Slow Train Coming* album, which together with the two that followed it, *Saved* and *Shot of Love*, are said to comprise Dylan's born-again Christian phase. Although the albums that follow these three no longer display lyrics formulated in distilled Christian terminology, they contain much to suggest that Dylan's form of Christianity cannot be dismissed as a mere passing phase. Many who dropped Dylan like a hot poker when he "turned Christian" later welcomed his newer songs with such comments as "Dylan is back." But Dylan answered to the effect that he was not ashamed he had told people how to save their souls but that it was time for him to do something else. After all, as he said, "Even Christ only preached for three years."

At any rate, there are two things that characterize Dylan's work from the beginning right up to the present: faith and The Lady. Indeed, the direction of development of his faith can be followed in all its subtleties and nakedness, especially in those songs where She appears.

On his first exclusively all-Dylan album, *The Freewheelin' Bob Dylan*, the first song is "Blowin' in the Wind." This song, perhaps the most famous Dylan song, is a plain and simple expression of the idea that the answer is to be found in the spirit, which like the wind, bloweth where it will. The second song, "Girl of the North Country," is a take off from an old English ballad. The last stanza is:

> So if you're travelin' in the north country fair
> Where the winds hit heavy on the borderline
> Remember me to one who lives there
> She once was a true love of mine

As a love ballad we need not see the girl of the north country as The Lady, yet because she lives up there where the winds hit heavy on the borderline, there is the suggestion of a threshold to be crossed in order to see or be with her. The poet of this song has been there at least once, and has known "true love." He therefore laments his estrangement. Many of Dylan's early folk songs are such laments or expressions of the struggle to regain his Lady-love.

Then in 1965 Dylan switched from the folk mode to rock and roll with his album, *Bringing It All Back Home*. On this album is the song "She Belongs to Me," which begins:

> She's got everything she needs
> She's an artist, she don't look back
> She's got everything she needs

The Return Of The Feminine

> She's an artist, she don't look back
> She can take the dark out of the nighttime
> And paint the daytime black

The next stanza tells us that although "you will start out standing, proud to steal her anything she sees ... you will wind up peeking through a keyhole down upon your knees." The male ego-principle will indeed start out proud but in the end will discover humility.

On this same album is another song in which The Lady figures prominently, "Love Minus Zero/No Limit":

> My love she speaks like silence
> Without ideals or violence
> She doesn't have to say she's faithful
> Yet she's true, like ice, like fire
> People carry roses
> Make promises by the hours
> My love she laughs like the flowers
> Valentines can't buy her

One could go on citing such examples and then proceed to discuss how each reveals aspects of inner struggle and transformation. But to do so would make this an overlong and awkward study. Instead, I would like to jump ahead to 1978 to a song called "Changing of The Guards." In this song, one can find an initiation, a revelation and a prophecy. Stanzas three and four express the initiation in terms that reflect the depth of Dylan's interior experience.

> The cold-blooded moon
> The captain waits above the celebration
> Sending his thoughts to a beloved maid

> Whose ebony face is beyond communication
> The captain is down but still believing that his love will be repaid
>
> They shaved her head
> She was torn between Jupiter and Apollo
> A messenger arrived with a black nightingale
> I seen her on the stairs and I couldn't help but follow
> Follow her down past the fountain where they lifted her veil

Dylan's next three albums are those of his so-called born-again Christian phase. On *Slow Train Coming*, there is "Precious Angel," which we have already discussed. Next, on *Saved*, there is "Covenant Woman":

> Covenant woman, intimate little girl
> Who knows those most secret things of me that are hidden from the world
> You know we are strangers in a land we're passing through.
> I'll always be right by your side, I've got a covenant too

Then on the *Shot Of Love* album, there is "In The Summertime." It may be that this song is addressed to The Lady, or it may also be understood as being addressed to Christ since the pronoun used is "you" and not "she":

> I was in your presence for an hour or so
> Or was it a day? I truly don't know

> Where the sun never set, where the trees hung low
> By that soft and shining sea

In stanza two:

> Fools, they made a mock of sin
> Our loyalty they tried to win
> But you were closer to me than my next of kin
> When they didn't want to know or see.

In stanza three:

> And I'm still carrying the gift you gave
> It's a part of me now; it's been cherished and saved
> It'll be with me unto the grave
> And then unto eternity

If this song is addressed to The Lady, then the gift she gave would be Dylan's creative genius. However, I tend to see this song as addressed to Christ and the gift He gave was The Lady herself, Dylan's feminine complement, which he will carry with him into eternity.

If the latter interpretation is correct, then the same idea is also found in the second verse of "Covenant Woman":

> I've been broken, shattered like an empty cup
> I'm just waiting on the Lord to rebuild and fill me up
> And I know he will do it 'cause He's faithful and He's true

> He must have loved me oh so much to send me someone as fine as you

Finally, on the *Infidels* album, which is considered to be post-"born-again" Dylan, there is "Sweetheart Like You." In the second verse:

> You know, I once knew a woman who looked like you
> She wanted a whole man, not just a half
> She used to call me sweet daddy when I was only a child
> You kind of remind me of her when you laugh

And the fourth verse:

> You know, news of you has come down the line
> Even before ya came in the door
> They say in your father's house, there's many mansions
> Each one of them got a fireproof floor
> Snap out of it, baby, people are jealous of you
> They smile to your face, but behind your back they hiss
> What's a sweetheart like you doin' in a dump like this?

In many of his lyrics, Dylan portrays the relationship between ordinary self-consciousness by which we experience ourselves as separate and isolated egos and that more intimate and inner consciousness of the soul through which we experience imaginatively and intuitively our inward connection to the – as Dylan once put it – "great wondrous melodious spirit which covereth the oneness of us all." This relationship, as an interior psychological drama with a mythological dimension, is expressed poetically in terms of the male and female within.

The return of the feminine is the return of the soul as the indispensable helpmate of the ego. When they have been joined together spiritually let no man put them asunder. The human being who has experienced this holy matrimony within himself has undergone a transformation of consciousness. He is not a mystic who turns his back on the world in order to bask in personal ecstasies. Rather, he is a visionary who, with the clear eye of the ego and the far-seeing eye of the soul, confronts the reality of existence with spiritual depth perception.

And so it is that I find in Dylan's work a vital and unique expression of the return of the feminine appropriate for our time. In this I see the true depth of his poetic vocation.

8

BOB DYLAN'S BLUES AND THE TWIN GODDESS

> If the soul had known God as perfectly as do the angels, it would never have entered the body. If the soul could have known God without the world, the world would never have been created. The world, therefore, was made for the soul's sake, so that the soul's eye might be practiced and strengthened to bear the divine light.
>
> -Meister Eckhart

In 1963 Dylan wrote a little ditty called "Bob Dylan's Blues." Its tone is one of folksy humor. But for the student of Dylan who approaches him with a believing soul, even a simple and humorous little song like this harbors hidden indications of Dylan's mystical, artistic journey through the world. Though it may easily be overlooked, there is a more serious undertone to this early Dylan song, which can throw a certain light upon his later development. The young folksinger, with tongue securely in cheek, sang:

> Well, the Lone Ranger and Tonto
> They are ridin' down the line
> Fixin' ev'rybody's troubles
> Ev'rybody's 'cept mine
> Somebody musta tol' 'em
> That I was doin' fine.

There is nothing more here than humor and the suggestion that Bob Dylan has troubles that even the legendary popular forces of good cannot fix. In the next stanza, the folksy humor continues. Yet beneath the surface a good deal more is suggested, in the form of understatement, about Dylan's essential perception of the spiritual, or more specifically, his idea of Wisdom as the object of his love:

> Oh you five and ten cent women
> With nothin' in your heads
> I got a real gal I'm lovin'
> And Lord I'll love her till I'm dead
> Go away from my door and my window too
> Right now

In the next stanza the folksy humor of the first stanza and the metaphorical suggestiveness of the second become more evenly balanced.

> Lord, I ain't goin' down to no race track
> See no sports car run
> I don't have no sports car
> And I don't even care to have one
> I can walk anytime around the block

The suggestion here is that living a fast and fashionable life, a life embedded in competition, is not something that interests him, and that one need not go far away to find out what such a life really has to offer. Then suddenly we are given a snap-shot image of the poet almost in terms of a cartoon character:

> Well, the wind keeps a-blowin' me
> Up and down the street
> With my hat in my hand
> And my boots on my feet
> Watch out so you don't step on me

He moves through the world (the street) directed by the spirit (the wind) with humility (hat in hand) and a certain amount of protection (boots). But he is aware of his own relative insignificance in this great big world, and he asks only that those around him not accidentally step on him.

If by this point in the song the artful play between the folksy humor and the metaphorical suggestiveness has not yet enticed you into a consideration of what is really being expressed, then you may have trouble figuring out how the last stanza fits with the song, or even why the song is called "Bob Dylan's Blues."

> Well, look it here buddy
> You want to be like me
> Pull out your six-shooter
> And rob every bank you can see
> Tell the judge I said it was all right
> Yes!

Dylan is not advocating that we all become outlaws, except maybe in the sense of the *Thief* in "All Along The Watchtower." It's certainly not all right to rob banks, but there are other kinds of "banks" in this day and age, caches of cultural and spiritual treasures from all past ages that have been hoarded or deposited in various books and people: veritable vaults of wisdom. If you want to be like Dylan, then you should take whatever you need from any of them. Spiritual treasures belong to no one, and you can help yourself. And you can tell the judge (God) for him, for Dylan, that what he has found based on this outlaw principle was "all right/Yes!"

The value of looking so closely at this little song is that it shows clearly how Dylan is able to express what is true for himself in a personal way, and yet do it in such a manner that on the surface the song can stand by itself as something pleasing and entertaining. At the personal center of this song, Dylan is saying this: I have my troubles, too, but they are the troubles of inner spiritual struggle, which the external forces of law and order, even those of legendary nobility, like the Lone Ranger and Tonto, cannot fix; Wisdom is the Woman I love; fashions are nowhere; my hat is always in my hand, but I can make it as long as I don't get crushed in the melee of traffic that is this world; to help me deal with my troubles, with *my blues*, I seek and find and take whatever I need from all the available vaults of spiritual wealth.

Of course, if you're not into all that, then "Bob Dylan's Blues" is just a humorous little ditty that you can tap your foot to, and laugh about. The interesting thing is that Dylan expresses what is in him, and sometimes it's entertaining for others whether they actually know what he's talking about or not. In this chapter, we shall see this again and again, and especially with a song like "Isis" which calls rather strongly upon a believing soul to be fully appreciated.

In the same year that he wrote "Bob Dylan's Blues," Dylan also wrote "Eternal Circle." This song was not released on a commercial album at the time, but as with many of his more intimate songs, its lyrics were published in the book *Writings and Drawings*, by Bob Dylan. It may be that this song was not recorded commercially because it was so predominately a personal song that it lacked the extra element of entertainment that would make it enjoyable to a wide audience. But, insofar as it is the inner spiritual and artistic mysteries of Dylan's career that interest us, we shall look at this "Eternal Circle." Before we do, however, I would like to offer some background considerations without which we would find the personal mystery of this song difficult to appreciate.

In the early days of Dylan's sky-rocketing career, a certain saying became strongly associated with him and became in fact the title of a film about his first British concert tour, "Don't Look Back." This is one of those sayings which may have many meanings and applications, but it's strongest allusion is to the Greek mysteries contained in the myth of Orpheus.

William Irwin Thompson wrote that myth "is itself a performance of the very reality it seeks to describe." The reality of myth, which is "the story of the soul," is the same reality as the mystery upon which life itself is founded. It is the reality of the cosmic, universal spirit that overlights this valley of the *shadow* of death. Man's consciousness of this higher and central reality has not always been the same.

In Greek mythology, Orpheus is said to be the son of the Muse, Calliope, and of Oeagrus, the Thracian River-God. According to Rudolf Steiner, this is an expression of the ancient Greek perception, arising out of an atavistic clairvoyance, of Orpheus' spiritual heritage, beside which the mundane facts of actual physical parentage are of little or no importance:

> The essential thing was the fact that he had within him – in his own field of experience – a quality derived from the supersensible world

and united with the material-physical element provided by his personality. The eyes of the Greeks were directed, not to the physical figure of Orpheus...this figure was more or less unessential, being merely the outer expression.... The essential element was what had descended from a supersensible source and had united with a material entity on the physical plane.

Steiner, as an initiate, also explained the more esoteric nature of the special form of consciousness that Orpheus experienced:

In the civilizations where ancient clairvoyance prevailed – and it was the same even among the Celts – when a man who was to be made aware of something he was called upon to communicate to his fellow men, it was revealed to him in this way: his etheric body emerged from the physical body and became the bearer of forces which streamed down into it. *If those who proclaimed the utterances of the spiritual world were men, their etheric bodies were female and they consequently saw in female form whatever communicated messages to them from spiritual worlds.*

Now it was also the purpose of the legend to show that although Orpheus was in direct contact with the spiritual Powers, as a son of a Thracian River-God there was always the possibility that he would be unable to retain what was revealed to him through his own etheric body. The more thoroughly he made himself at home in the physical world and lived his life as a son of his country, the more did his powers of clairvoyance recede. The story relates that Eurydice, the transmitter of his revelations, *his soul-bride*, was torn away from him through the bite of an adder – a picture of his human failings – and carried off to the underworld. He could win her back by passing through an Initiation – whenever we are told of a journey to the underworld, an Initiation is meant. In order to win back his bride, Orpheus must pass through an initiation. But he was already too closely enmeshed in the physical world. He had indeed acquired the capacity to make his way into the underworld, but on his return, when his eyes again encountered the sunlight, Eurydice vanished from his sight. Why was this? It was because on seeing the sunlight he did something that was forbidden him: he turned and looked back.

...with a nature still rooted in the spiritual he is also, partially, the sort of being which it is his destiny to become on the physical plane. And so all the forces of the physical plane press in upon him and he loses Eurydice, *his own innocent soul – which is the fate of modern man also to lose*. (Emphasis added)

The fate of modern man is that he was destined, like Orpheus, to lose his innocent soul, his soul-bride. She must remain in the underworld, the spiritual world, until he has proven his trust in the spirit by not looking back. In the esoteric view, the atavistic clairvoyance that was man's natural early endowment had to recede into the background while ego-consciousness grew strong, and that at some point in the future the clairvoyance will return without the loss of ego-consciousness. "The return of the feminine" is in some sense the return of the soul as the agent of clairvoyance, of the feminine complement of the "male" ego, to establish a spiritual harmonic reunion of imagination and will.

This return process is a large and gradual movement reflecting a change in the relationship of the physical and spiritual worlds within the developing consciousness of mankind. On this level, the astral and etheric together form the feminine soul-principle. However, the etheric body apart from the astral takes the opposite form of the physical body in which it is incarnated. For a man, the etheric body takes the feminine form; for a woman, the male form. But to experience one's own etheric body as a matter of inner visionary experience already indicates an uncommon degree of initiation into the mysteries of the spirit. The myth of Orpheus, as a description of spiritual reality, is at the same time a performance of the reality it describes. The innocent soul of the human being remains in the underworld when he incarnates in a physical body on earth. To regain that innocent soul, one must enter the underworld, or undergo initiation. On the level of individual visionary experience what a woman beholds might be called "a god," and what a man beholds might be called "a goddess."

As that larger movement we have called the return of the feminine progresses, it might be reasonable to expect that more and more human beings will have inner experiences of their own individual male and female complements. At any rate, something like this inner experience of the individual etheric body emerging from the physical in visionary experience seems to be what Dylan expressed in his song "Eternal Circle":

> I sang the song slowly
> As she stood in the shadows

> She stepped to the light
> As my silver strings spun
> She called with her eyes
> To the tune I's a-playin'
> But the song it was long
> And I'd only begun

She moves from the shadows into the light as his silver strings spun. She calls with her eyes to the tune he's playing. Throughout this song "she" is portrayed in such mysterious ways as to suggest her living connected-ness with the song itself.

> Through the bullet of light
> Her face was reflectin'
> The fast fading words
> That rolled from my tongue
> With a long-distance look
> Her eyes was on fire
> But the song it was long
> And there was more to be sung

Her intimate connection with the song he is singing is expressed again in that the words are reflected in her face. That she has a "long distance" look and that her eyes are on fire hints that this is no physical form.

> My eyes dance a circle
> Across her clear outline
> With her head tilted sideways
> She called me again
> As the tune drifted out
> She breathed hard through the echo

> But the song it was long
> And it was far to the end

She beckons to him with a gesture as the tune drifts out, and it is she who mysteriously breathes hard *through* the echo.

> I glanced at my guitar
> And played it pretendin'
> That of all the eyes out there
> I could see none
> As her thoughts pounded hard
> Like the pierce of an arrow
> But the song it was long
> And it had to get done

Somehow he is aware of *her* thoughts pounding hard. There is the suggestion that it is her thoughts that are entering him as arrows, which then come out as "the song."

> As the tune finally folded
> I laid down the guitar
> Then looked for the girl
> Who'd stayed for so long
> But her shadow was missin'
> For all of my searchin'
> So I picked up my guitar
> And began the next song

That it is her shadow that is missing suggests again that this is not a physical form he is talking about. If this were simply a song about a girl in the audience who catches his eye while he is performing, it would be a completely inconsequential creation. But with all of the unusual and mysterious phrasings and with the title, "Eternal Circle," one suspects there is something more being expressed. The fact that she disappears the minute he puts his guitar down – which only moves him to pick it up again to start another song – suggests that she is only present *in the performance* of the creative act. The "eternal circle" is not only the eternal round of performing in order to bring about her appearance, but even more it is the connection made with the eternal during the act of creation. In the act of creation her presence connects him with the eternal from which his artistic inspirations come. They come to *him* through *her*. As the poet Robert Graves once famously put it, "Woman is, man does."

One year later, in 1964, Dylan recorded "Spanish Harlem Incident." This song, like "Eternal Circle," is about Dylan's inner experience of his own innocent soul or etheric soul-bride who brings to him the inspirations for his art. However, this song, as it was recorded, can be enjoyed as an intensely passionate love song without an appreciation for its inner personal dimension. The initial *conceit* of this song is that the "girl" is a fortune-teller he consults to find out about his future. But if one were to stick too closely to that conceit, the song as a whole would be incomprehensible.

> Gypsy gal, the hands of Harlem
> Cannot hold you to its heat
> Your temperature's too hot for taming
> Your flaming feet burn up the street
> I am homeless, come and take me
> Into reach of your rattling drums
> Let me know, babe, about my fortune
> Down along my restless palms

To ask about his fortune down along his restless palms, while suggesting palm-reading, is really to ask about his fortune as a creative, performing artist.

> Gypsy gal, you got me swallowed
> I have fallen far beneath
> Your pearly eyes, so fast an' slashing
> An' your flashing diamond teeth.
> The night is pitch black, come and make my
> Pale face fit into place, ah, please!
> Let me know, babe, I'm nearly drowning
> If it's you my life lines trace

Always the man with his hat in his hands, he knows that it is all up to her. He would like confirmation, however, that he is on the right track and that she is really the one that his life is all about.

> I been wonderin' all about me
> Ever since I seen you there
> On the cliffs of your wildcat charms I'm riding
> I know I'm round you but I don't know where
> You have slayed me, you have made me
> I got to laugh halfways off my heels
> I got to know, babe, will you surround me
> So I can tell if I'm really real

He's in her vicinity, but he's not quite sure where. Her presence as an inner vision is not automatic. Sometimes he can see her, but sometimes he can only sense her presence. He has to wonder about himself with all these unusual inner experiences. But finally he realizes that in slaying him she has made him, and he can't help but laugh out in ecstatic relief at this realization. Still, he longs to see her again, because only then can he feel quite real.

In "Bob Dylan's Blues" the "real gal" that he loves and will love till he's dead is Wisdom or Sophia. But in "Eternal Circle" and "Spanish Harlem Incident," the woman is personified in a more intimate way as his own soul-bride. In terms of ancient mythology, Sophia is the Mother while Psyche, the soul-bride, is the Maiden. In the Neolithic culture of Catal Huyuk, what we might call Sophia and Psyche and what the Greeks called Demeter and Persephone, were perceived together and called the Twin Goddess. Describing a statue from the pre-historic culture of Catal Huyuk, William Irwin Thompson wrote, "On the one side we see the Great Mother with her infant, on the other we see the Great Mother in embrace with her lover. The two females are back to back and are really one body, and in each case, the female is larger than the male."

The Mother, Sophia, and the Maid, Psyche, are only separate entities as abstract concepts. Within the unity of spiritual life they are indivisible. This condition of the inner life can sometimes make it difficult to interpret many of Dylan's lyrics in a precise way. It may be clear enough to him because it is his experience. But the language used to convey such profound inner experiences remains somewhat obscure for those of us who have not yet journeyed so far inward.

In 1975 Dylan wrote another song, which like "Eternal Circle," was not recorded on a commercial album. It was published, however, in *Lyrics 1962-1985,* an updated version of *Writings and Drawings*. This song, "Golden Loom," much like "Eternal Circle," seems too intensely personal to have warranted release as a regular recording. But this mystical and esoteric lyric can add to our appreciation of Dylan's personal artistic quest.

> Smokey autumn night, stars up in the sky
> I see the sailin' boats across the bay go by
> Eucalyptus trees hang above the street
> And then I turn my head, for you're approachin' me
> Moonlight on the water, fisherman's daughter, floatin' into my room
> With a golden loom

Amid the serenity of an autumn night, she, "the fisherman's daughter," floats into the room of his consciousness, bringing her golden loom. In the male-female dichotomy of personal consciousness, the fisherman's daughter could be the off-spring of Christ-consciousness, a Christic-daughter, as it were, born of Sophia.

> First we wash our feet near the immortal shrine
> And then our shadows meet and then we drink the wine
> I see the hungry clouds up above your face
> And then the tears roll down, what a bitter taste
> And then you drift away on a summer's day where the wildflowers bloom
> With your golden loom

This is a mystical ceremony of cleansing and sacrifice. Although it was an autumn night when she floated in, it is a summer day when she drifts away. This change from night to day and from autumn to summer is not an indication of the length of her stay, but an indication of a translation of Dylan's consciousness to a different and inner landscape. It is where the wildflowers bloom from her golden loom.

> I walk across the bridge in the dismal light
> Where all the cars are stripped between the gates of night
> I see the trembling lion with the lotus flower tail
> And then I kiss your lips as I lift your veil
> But you're gone and then all I seem to recall is the smell of perfume
> And your golden loom

Now that he is on the inner planes, he follows her across the bridge to the other side of night. The cars that are stripped before crossing are the physical bodies stripped away from the soul. The "trembling lion with the lotus flower tail" would suggest to an occultist the chakras or inner centers of the subtle or etheric body, which, as it is said, reverse their motion and appear to whirl during initiation. He kisses his soul-bride as he lifts her veil, but suddenly she is gone. He is left merely with a memory of perfume and of her golden loom.

It is interesting that this song comes chronologically just before the release of the *Street Legal* album because all the songs on *Street Legal* are about initiatory kinds of experience.

Dylan wrote a great many other songs in ballad form that can be appreciated as having hidden expressions of the inner relationship to the Twin Goddess of Sophia/Psyche. Among them are "Sara," "Simple Twist of Fate," "If You See Her, Say Hello," "Tangled Up In Blue," "You're Gonna Make Me Lonesome When You Go," "Never Say Goodbye," "Tough Mama," "You Angel, You," "Hazel," "Isis," and "Up To Me." In many of these songs the relationship is balladized, or told in the form of a story, and so they have that extra element of entertainment. One such song, "Isis," I would like to look at to round out this study of Dylan and the Twin Goddess.

"Isis," co-authored with Jacque Levy, was published the same year as "Golden Loom." It is a ballad that paints a vivid picture of the mystical marriage to Isis, the Twin Goddess Sophia/Psyche. The drama underlying this event is an inner adventure, or more accurately, a misadventure, since it tells the story of a temptation that confronts every traveler on the inner planes. We will look at the story this song tells by dividing it up into three sections of four stanzas each, and then the final stanza by itself. The first stanza begins immediately with the marriage to Isis on the fifth day of May stated simply as a fact. It is important to note the peculiar construction of this song: it begins and ends on the fifth day of May, which indicates that the story itself takes place outside of time.

> I married Isis on the fifth day of May
> But I could not hold onto her very long
> So I cut off my hair and I rode straight away
> For the wild unknown country where I could not go wrong
>
> I came to a high place of darkness and light
> The dividing line ran through the center of town
> I hitched up my pony to a post on the right
> Went into a laundry to wash my clothes down
>
> A man in the corner approached me for a match
> I knew right away he was not ordinary
> He said, "Are you lookin' for somethin' easy to catch?"
> I said, "I got no money." He said, "That ain't necessary"

> We set out that night for the cold in the North
> I gave him my blanket, he gave me his word
> I said, "Where are we goin'?" He said we be back by the fourth
> I said, "That's the best news that I've ever heard"

On the other side of the threshold time is experienced as space. In the eternal, which means outside of time, time itself is experienced, to quote Thompson again, as "gathered up into a single space of consciousness." So the news that they will be back by the fourth is indeed very good news to him. He will return in time to re-experience that eternal moment of the fifth day of May.

When he arrives at the high place where darkness and light are evenly balanced, he makes the decision to tie up his pony, his consciousness, to the *right* side, the side of light. Then comes a purification, a cleansing: His clothes are the outer sheaths of his being, the physical, etheric and astral bodies. During this process of purification he is approached by someone who is not ordinary, someone who offers him the temptation of "something easy to catch." They then set out for the cold in the North.

> I was thinkin' about turquoise, I was thinkin' about gold
> I was thinkin' about diamonds and the world's biggest necklace
> As we rode through the canyons, through the devilish cold
> I was thinkin' about Isis, how she thought I was so reckless

How she told me that one day we would meet up again
And things would be different the next time we wed
If I only could hang on and just be her friend
I still can't remember all the best things she said

We came to the pyramids all embedded in ice
He said, "there's a body I'm trying to find
If I carry it out it'll bring a good price"
'Twas then that I knew what he had on his mind

The wind it was howlin' and the snow was outrageous
We chopped through the night and we chopped through the dawn
When he died I was hopin' that it wasn't contagious
But I made up my mind that I had to go on

This is a temptation not unlike the temptation of Christ when he is offered the world by Satan. In the modern esoteric world-view revealed in the work of Rudolf Steiner, it is said that a man can cross the threshold into the spiritual world in two directions. One is the expansion of the soul out into the Cosmos, the Great World of the Macrocosm, and the other is a concentration or compression of the ego into and through the microcosm of one's own hidden spiritual being. Although we undergo both of these processes daily, we do so unconsciously. The crossing of the threshold in either direction as a matter of *conscious* experience entails dangers for which one must be prepared. When we go to sleep and our soul expands out into the Macrocosm, we sink into unconsciousness, and on the return into the Microcosm of our own spiritual being our faculty of conscious attention is diverted immediately to the world of sense-perception, which acts as a sort of veil covering the depths of our spiritual being. From the point of view of the initiate who can consciously enter the spiritual world, the world of sense-perception is a world of Maya or illusion, *but it is a world of illusion with a beneficent purpose*: to protect the unprepared soul until it has become practiced and strengthened enough to bear the divine light.

In ancient cultures, initiations were directed by trained hierophants who could assist the neophyte within the safe and secluded sanctuary of the Mystery Temples. This was a secret and sacred undertaking. But in the long evolution of man, things have gradually changed. As the inner and hidden spiritual being of man changes, his relationship as a physical being to the spiritual world also changes. From the dawn of time to the coming of Christ, initiation within Mystery Temples became increasingly more difficult, eventually dying out as a viable possibility.

But the life, death and resurrection of Christ, properly understood, was an enactment upon the open stage of history of the mysteries of initiation, which are henceforth removed from the guarded secretiveness of Mystery Temples. The hour comes, and perhaps now is, when man will be able to cross the threshold consciously by using Christ's life, death and resurrection as his model and guide. This is part of the esoteric meaning of "Blessed are the poor in spirit, for theirs is the kingdom of heaven." The poor in spirit are the "beggars for the spirit" who will in time, with their "hats in their hands," find the kingdom of heaven by going into and through the mysteries of their own being, guided by the example of Christ. When Christ ascended, he said that we would see him return, coming in the clouds. The second coming, rather than being a physical return of Christ, is the reappearance of Christ to those who cross the threshold by going into and through their own hidden being. This is the "changing of the guards" which requires inner courage.

For in modern initiation, even as in ancient initiation, the soul necessarily experiences trials and temptations for which it must prepare itself. The initiation through the microcosm of one's own inner being involves a certain "anointing" or cleansing to purge us of the stubborn egoisms lurking in the depths of our being.

In this descent into the microcosm, we are met by Lucifer or Diabolus, whose function or job is to tempt us, as he did Christ, by offering us the world. We may find ourselves thinking about diamonds and gold and the world's largest necklace. But these temptations are the products of the passions and desires that rise up out of the depths of our own egotistic being to confront us. They are our own projections, illusions, maya. This tempter, this man that you will know right away is not ordinary, will offer you what *you* want from the egotistic depths of your being. But it is all illusion, and if we have prepared ourselves by concentration on the life of Christ and by trying to live that life, we will find the inner strength to say, "Get thee behind me." The body that the tempter is trying to find is the body of our spiritual being, our spiritual body-being. If he captures it, he will have been paid, but we will have lost ourselves in the process. The struggle of our engagement with him we will be a chopping through the night to reach the dawn. We must hold on as a friend of Isis, of Sophia, of Wisdom, and make up our mind to go on.

> I broke into the tomb, but the casket was empty
> There was no jewels, no nothin', I felt I'd been had

When I saw that my partner was just bein'
friendly
When I took up his offer I must-a been mad

I picked up his body and I dragged him inside
Threw him down in the hole and I put back
the cover
I said a quick prayer and I felt satisfied
Then I rode back to find Isis just to tell her
I love her

She was there in the meadows where the creek
used to rise
Blinded by sleep and in need of a bed
I came in from the east with the sun in my eyes
I cursed her one time then I rode on ahead

She said, "Where ya been?" I said, "No place
special"
She said, "You look different." I said, "Well,
I guess"
She said, "You been gone." I said, "That's only
natural"
She said, "You gonna stay?" I said, "If you want
me to, yes"

The physical body is the tomb of the spirit. To break into the tomb is to pierce the veil of sense-perception and to enter into the hidden spiritual reality underlying the body. After experiencing this inner drama of temptation as a part of the initiatory process, it is possible to see that your "partner" was just being friendly, since this inner trial is necessary before crossing the threshold. Now, it is also possible to see that when you took up his offer you must have been mad – impassioned by pure egotism. But once you are past him, you can say a quick prayer and feel satisfied. Now completely stripped of self-desires, you have only to return to Isis just to tell her you love her.

In *Ecclesiasticus* it is written of Wisdom:

> She walks with him as a stranger, and at first she puts him to the test; fear and dread she brings upon him and tries him with her discipline; and with her precepts she puts him to the proof, until his heart is fully with her. Then she comes back to bring him happiness and reveal her secrets to him.

She puts him to the proof until his heart is fully with her. So, as he comes in from the east with the sun in his eyes, he curses her one time because of the "hell" she has put him through. But then he rides on ahead because now his heart is fully with her. He is different now, naturally, after this trial. Will he stay this time? If *She* wants him to, yes.

This song is a dramatization of interior, spiritual experience and as such it takes place out of time or perhaps in "existential time." The poet, however, returns to normal consciousness and to the world of time to compose his work of art. And so, in the last stanza, the poet has returned and recalls the whole experience:

> Isis, oh Isis, you mystical child
> What drives me to you is what drives me insane
> I still can remember the way that you smiled
> On the fifth day of May in the drizzlin' rain

In the early days of his career, Dylan sang in "The Times They Are A-Changin'":

> Come gather 'round people
> Wherever you roam
> And admit that the waters
> Around you have grown

In the same year, he sang in "When the Ship Comes In":

> For the chains of the sea
> Will have busted in the night
> And will be buried at the bottom of the ocean

And more recently and more intensely on the *Street Legal* album, he sang:

> But Eden is burning, either get ready for elimination
> Or else your hearts must have the courage for the changing of the guards

The "changing of the guards" is a changing of man's relationship to the spiritual world. Many so-called "new-age" commentators as well as such writers and thinkers as Nicolas Berdyaev, Henry Miller, Thomas Merton and William Irwin Thompson have recognized that in some sense mankind as a whole is approaching a crossing of the threshold as we move into the post-modern era. That crossing entails an intensification and expansion of personal consciousness. Dylan's poetry seems especially important as an artistic reflection and expression of this historic process.

The more subtle aspects of Dylan's art cannot be fully comprehended or appreciated without some awareness of the esoteric knowledge now making its way into post-industrial culture. For that reason, I have made use of that knowledge as a way of suggesting the wider dimensions of Dylan's art and the nature of his spiritual perceptions. Some of Dylan's songs, such as "Isis" and "Golden Loom" and "Changing of the Guards," reveal an esoteric quality in his mystical approach to the mystery upon which life is founded.

9

THE JOURNEY THROUGH DARK HEAT

> ...the divine god in every person, through the Fall, becomes encased in an ego and held in place in a society of other egos. When our better half, our divine goddess, Isis, comes down in search of us, we are so dead that we cannot recognize her or remember where we came from ... she does not enter time on the terms of the ego.
>
> -William Irwin Thompson

In Bob Dylan's mythopoeic manner of expression, women represent the soul/imaginational side of our being while men represent the ego/will element. But the ego, before the metanoiac experience of conversion, is merely a *Joker*. After that conversion he undergoes a gradual process of inner self-development to become reborn as a "prince" within the unity of the holy spirit. In a sense, the *Joker* is the Old Adam of Pauline Christianity within us, while the reborn ego is the New Adam, which is wed to its spiritual bride, and therefore made whole, or holy, in the image of Christ, Whose Being, as the archetypal consummate individual, is comprised of both the Logos and Sophia.

But this transformation, this spiritual rebirth, is a process requiring time, both for the individual and for mankind as a whole. In the work of Teilhard de Chardin, for example, creation is viewed as a process that is still on-going, which has not yet reached completion. Chardin sees "cosmosgenesis," the becoming of the world, as a slow, maturational process that is inwardly guided toward its culmination by the gradual and eventual fulfillment of Christ, or "Christogenesis," in time. These two processes come together at the end of time as the "Parousia," a Greek word that means "beyond or through being." It points toward the actual and yet spiritual completion of the creation of man and his world. Chardin calls this total process the "Pleromization" because Pleroma means fullness or plentitude, and he sees this process as the gradual extension of Christ's redemptive power working in and through evolutionary movements into all the multiplicity of the physical world. The eventual transformation of individual souls who then come together in higher consciousness is a part of the long evolutionary movement toward Parousia.

Something like this gradual, evolutionary development is what Dylan expresses with the idea of the "Slow Train" – "the holy slow train" – as he called it back in 1965 on the liner notes for *Highway 61 Revisited*. The album titled *Slow Train Coming*, which came out in 1979, is generally regarded as the work that marks Dylan's debut as a Christian. Indeed, this album caught many of his fans by surprise, even shocking those who were inclined to view this so-called conversion as some sort of betrayal. This negative reaction to Dylan's Christianity was due, at least in part, to an erroneous perception of it as a conventional kind of fundamentalist "born-again" conversion. In this chapter, we hope to show that although Dylan's

Christianity began long before the release of *Slow Train Coming*, the fervor and uncanny directness of the lyrics on that album, and on the two that followed it, have their source not in fundamentalist doctrines, but in the personal mystical experiences of initiation recorded on the *Street Legal* album.

In 1964 Dylan sang in a song called "Restless Farewell":

> But the dark does die
> As the curtain is drawn and somebody's eyes
> Must meet the dawn

In this same song he also said:

> But it's not to go naked under unknowin' eyes
> It's for myself and my friends my stories are sung

Dylan, intent on meeting the dawn, intent on attaining spiritual transformation, has directed his creative efforts to giving artistic expression to the naked moments of this process of transformation within the soul. He does this firstly for himself and secondarily for his friends, those similarly concerned with meeting the dawn. That his artistic journey of spiritual transformation led him to an inner experience of Christian mysteries confounded many.

In 1978 Dylan released *Street Legal*. This album, in many respects, is one of the crowning achievements of his long and prolific career. Heavily laden with personal and esoteric imagery, it reveals a man with considerable inner experience at the threshold. Aside from showing the deep mystical foundations of Dylan's Christianity, it also indicates a certain milestone in the development of his interior life. For this reason it begins, in the first song, "Changing of the Guards," on a personal, autobiographical note:

> Sixteen years
> Sixteen banners united over the field
> Where the good shepherd grieves
> Desperate men, desperate women divided
> Spreading their wings 'neath the falling leaves
>
> Fortune calls
> I stepped forth from the shadows, to the marketplace
> Merchants and thieves, hungry for power, my last deal gone down
> She's smelling sweet like the meadows where she was born
> On midsummer's eve, near the tower

If we go back 16 years from *Street Legal* to 1962, we can find a song called "Long Ago, Far Away," which may be the earliest indication in Dylan's work of a Christian element. The song begins and ends with this:

> To preach of peace and brotherhood
> Oh, what might be the cost!
> A man he did it long ago
> And they hung him on a cross
> Long ago, far away
> Things like that don't happen
> No more, nowadays, (do they?)

In any event, 1962 was the year Dylan's first record was released, and so he had been at his task for 16 years when *Street Legal* came out. His 16 years of dedication to his artistic quest culminates in the experience of the initiation that is expressed in "Changing of the Guards."

In Chapter Seven, I remarked on the fact that the initiation recorded in "Changing of the Guards" was expressed in terms of "a beloved maid/Whose ebony face is beyond communication," and that he followed her, his soul-bride, "down past the fountain where they lifted her veil." During this initiation, he receives a kind of revelation and makes a kind of prophecy expressed in the last few stanzas. When this beloved maid is "begging to know what measures he (God) now will be taking," she receives this response:

> Gentlemen, he said
> I don't need your organization, I've shined your shoes
> I've moved your mountains and marked your cards
> But Eden is burning, either get ready for elimination
> Or else your hearts must have the courage for the changing of the guards

God doesn't need man-made organizations. He's shined our shoes, that is, given us what we need to walk the path, the natural dignity of our humanity in the likeness and image of God. He's performed miracles, and though we all play with less than a full deck, the cards have been marked in such a way that if we really want to find the truth, we can. But Eden, the transcendental spiritual home of our existentiality, is burning. The time has come to rise above what we have been, to transform ourselves, to change our consciousness. Then comes the prophecy:

> Peace will come
> With tranquility and splendor on the wheels of fire
> But will bring us no reward when her false idols fall
> And cruel death surrenders with its pale ghost retreating
> Between the King and Queen of Swords

Thus, *Street Legal* begins with a poetic expression of a mystical initiation. Except for the reference to the "good shepherd" in the first stanza, there is little to suggest that this was a specifically Christian initiation. But I will look at two more songs from this album, and one of these, "Señor," should make it clear that Dylan's was a Christian initiation. We have already shown in previous chapters that hidden references to Christ were made in the songs "Like A Rolling Stone" and "Visions of Johanna." Other early songs could be cited as well, such as "I'd Hate to Be You on That Dreadful Day" (1964), and "Bob Dylan's 115th Dream" (1965). There is also the mysterious refrain from "Sad-Eyed Lady of the Lowlands," an autobiographical song about contemplating suicide:

> Sad-eyed lady of the lowlands
> Where the sad-eyed prophet says that no man comes
> My warehouse eyes, my Arabian drums
> Should I put them by your gate
> Or, sad-eyed lady, should I wait?

The "sad-eyed prophet," like the "one-eyed undertaker," cannot believe in the coming of the man of humanity, the Christ. The mind of such a self, its feminine complement, could be construed as "the sad-eyed lady of the lowlands." That is the kind of mindset that may descend heavily upon one in moments of doubt.

There is also the curious song Dylan wrote in 1968 called variously "Quinn the Eskimo" or "The Mighty Quinn." Quinn could be understood as a sobriquet for Christ, if we consider the last four lines:

> But when Quinn the Eskimo gets here
> Ev'rybody's gonna wanna doze
> Come on without, come on within
> You'll not see nothing like the mighty Quinn

That curious line about everybody wanting to doze when the mighty Quinn gets here suggests that everyone will want to sleep in Christ, in the mystical sense of being asleep to one's egotistical nature while awakened to Christ-consciousness. Sleeping or dying in Christ is the effective death of the ego in which one is alive to Christ as the existential basis of his own real being and can say with St. Paul: "Not I, but Christ lives in me."

In the same year, 1968, Dylan released "I Dreamed I Saw St. Augustine" which is on the same album as "All Along The Watchtower." St. Augustine is seen "searching for the very souls/Whom already have been sold," sold in the New Testament sense, which Dylan echoed on the *Saved* album with: "He bought me with a price." After this vision of St. Augustine, it is simply astounding that so many were nevertheless surprised when Dylan started singing overtly Christian lyrics in

1979. But the interesting thing is that it was St. Augustine that Dylan saw, for it was this Bishop of Hippo who wrote:

> What we now call the Christian religion already existed among the ancients, and was not lacking at the very beginning of the human race. When Christ appeared in the flesh, the true religion already in existence received the name of Christianity.

For Dylan's Christianity rises above mere names and sectarianism to the eternal: "That solid rock/Made before the foundation of the world." It is not one of the weekend varieties, but a mystically consuming way of life. However much Christian fundamentalism and Dylan's Christianity may have in common, there is in Dylan's not only the recognition that "I don't need your organization," but also a foundation in the esoteric mysticism so prevalent on *Street Legal*. Consider the second song on *Street Legal* called "New Pony":

> Once I had a pony, her name was Lucifer
> I had a pony, her name was Lucifer
> She broke her leg and needed shooting
> I swear it hurt me more than it could ever have hurted her

In esoteric literature there is a particular relationship between horses and human intelligence. It is said that animal forms evolved, in a certain sense, out of the human, and that the forces of all the animals exist in some way within the human being. It is said that at the time in man's evolution when he became an intelligent creature, the forces that entered into him to produce this intelligence also manifested correspondingly in the world of nature as "the horse," so that there exists within the mystery of life an inner affinity between man as an intelligent being and the appearance of the horse. This affinity is the basis for the old sayings about having "good horse sense," and for man's long and close association with the horse. This esoteric understanding of the evolution of animal forms is hinted at in Dylan's "Man Gave Names to All the Animals," which appears on the *Slow Train Coming* album.

The horse, therefore, is the right corresponding symbol to use as an image of intelligence. In "New Pony" Dylan says that his old form of intelligence was a Luciferic intelligence, and as it proved too lame to carry him where he needed to go, he had to kill it. The accomplishment of this painful task hurt him more than it could have Lucifer. The fact that his old horse, "Lucifer," is a "she" instead of "he" is in keeping with the recognition that aspects of soul are feminine while aspects of will are masculine.

This mythopoeic consciousness of the male and female of personal consciousness instills many of the songs on the unreservedly Christian *Slow Train Coming* album with potent cryptic expressions that also point beyond the usual range of conventional Christianity. For instance, in the title song "Slow Train," we find the following strident stanza that is full of riddles that depend on understanding the male-female dichotomy of personal consciousness, if they are to be resolved:

> Big-time negotiators, false healers and woman haters
> Masters of the bluff and masters of the proposition
> But the enemy I see
> Wears a cloak of decency

> All non-believers and men stealers talkin' in
> the name of religion
> And there's a slow, slow train comin' up around
> the bend

The riddles contained in this lyric reveal an Emersonian sensibility. The fact that the enemy Dylan sees wears a cloak of "decency" calls to mind Emerson's indictment of our American culture at the end of his famous Harvard address of 1837, "The American Scholar":

> The spirit of the American freeman is already suspected to be timid, imitative, tame. Public and private avarice makes the air we breath thick and fat. The scholar is *decent*, indolent, complaisant. (Emphasis added)

The American scholar in being decent, as here understood, means *conforming to approved social standards* rather than striving to "Let the grandeur of justice shine in his affairs." With his eye on success instead of truth, the American scholar yields to "the vulgar prosperity that retrogrades ever to barbarism."

There may be masters of the bluff and masters of the proposition, but the enemies Dylan zeros in on as hiding behind decency are "non-believers" and "men stealers" talking in the name of religion. "Woman haters" are those who hate the soul and the imagination. Emerson said, "The one thing in the world of value, is the active soul," and going further, "The one fact the world hates, that the soul *becomes*." "Non-believers" who talk in the name of religion but do not conceive the soul as dynamically capable of development, would bind us with formulas and dogmas and become thereby "men stealers," stripping us of our free-will.

The Journey Through Dark Heat

One of the central concerns of Emerson's thought is self-trust. In "Self-Reliance," he wrote: "Trust thyself: every heart vibrates to that iron strong." "Great men," he wrote, "have always ... confided themselves childlike to the genius of their age, betraying their perception that the absolute trustworthy was seated at their heart, working through their hands, predominating in all their being." The genius of this age is involved with the crossing of the threshold, and so Dylan's Christianity has a strong link with esotericism. But even in this he remains as ever, "freewheelin'." In "When You Gonna Wake Up?" on the *Slow Train Coming* album, he sings:

> Spiritual advisors and gurus to guide your every move
> Instant inner peace and every step you take has got to be approved
>
> When you gonna wake up, when you gonna wake up
> When you gonna wake up and strengthen the things that remain?

In all this there is the conviction that in a certain sense one must "go it alone," one must go into his chamber and pray in private. Perhaps this explains why the full title of "Señor" on the *Street Legal* album is "Señor (Tales of Yankee Power)." This title, by echoing the title of Carlos Castaneda's book, *Tales of Power*, points to this song as a story of inner transformation. The word "yankee" carries the interesting connotations of both "free-booter" and being from the "north country." If we think of a yankee as being a kind of pioneering spirit who braves the frontiers on his own, then in Dylan's song we have the picture of the pioneering spirit exploring the frontiers of mystical transformation. Here is yet another experience on the threshold where the poet is knocking on heaven's door. The song itself, however, takes the form of a prayer, spoken in the privacy of one's own chamber, to Christ who is addressed, as He is in Spanish, "the loving tongue," as "Señor":

> Señor, señor, can you tell me where we're headin'?
> Lincoln County Road or Armageddon?
> Seems like I been down this way before
> Is there any truth in that, señor?

Are we on the road to emancipation or on the road to destruction? It all seems so familiar, have I not been here before? Is there any truth to reincarnation? The questioning continues in the next stanza within the context of the feminine complement.

> Señor, señor, do you know where she's hidin'?
> How long are we gonna be ridin'?
> How long must I keep my eyes glued to the door?
> Will there be any comfort there, señor?

Where is "she" and how long will this torment go on? How long must I go on contemplating my own death and is it true, will there be any comfort there? At this point, he begins to take stock of his situation, perceived in the poetic images of the next two stanzas:

> There's a wicked wind still blowin' on that upper deck

The Journey Through Dark Heat

> There's an iron cross still hanging down from around her neck
> There's a marchin' band still playin' in that vacant lot
> Where she held me in her arms one time and said, "Forget me not"
>
> Señor, señor, I can see that painted wagon
> I can smell the tail of the dragon
> Can't stand the suspense anymore
> Can you tell me who to contact here, señor?

He realizes that there is still an evil spirit at work in the mind and that the physical body, with the iron of self-will still coursing through it, hangs down from "her" neck, from the soul, like a cross. The marching band of militarism still calls the tune in this vacant lot of a world where "she" once held him in her mystical embrace. He sees the earth as a colorful cosmic wagon carrying us all along through space. At the same time he is all too aware, as if through the intimate sense of smell, of the dragon, of those evil forces that infest the earth. He can't stand the suspense of this cosmic and spiritual conflict any longer and longs to know the outcome, but who knows that? Is there anyone he could contact here to find out?

Then, on the recording, there is an instrumental musical interlude during which these lyrics echo within the listener as he ponders the experience of this song. When the singing resumes, we are plunged straight away into the mystical experience in which the "yankee" goes into the frontier, naked and alone.

> Well, the last thing I remember before I stripped and kneeled

> Was that trainload of fools bogged down in a
> magnetic field
> A gypsy with a broken flag and a flashing ring
> Said, "Son, this ain't a dream no more, it's the
> real thing"
>
> Señor, señor, you know their hearts is as hard
> as leather
> Well, give me a minute, let me get it together
> I just gotta pick myself up off the floor
> I'm ready when you are, señor

This is a poetic rendering of an ineffable initiatory experience. The gypsy with his broken flag and flashing ring is something like what esotericists refer to as the "guardian of the threshold." That guardian is a being encountered on the inner planes of experience who keeps us from crossing the threshold until we are ready. In the inner mysteries of being, he is a visionary representation created by our own higher spiritual being to hold us back until we are ready. His flag, his trick of waving us off to keep us from crossing, is broken and the awakened individual consciousness crosses the threshold, entering the spiritual world. Here, what may be experienced no longer qualifies as mere dreamy visionary experience, but is spiritually real.

Stars, the stars we behold at night when looking into the sky, are the external symbols of the spirit world, the world of light, from which man has fallen and to which he longs to return. But the return involves initiation and transformation. To the extent that Dylan's poetry concerns itself with spiritual transformation it may be said to be a "poetry of the stars." Rabindranath Tagore, writing about how the stars can speak to us as we gaze up at them in the night, revealing to us the "infinite personality" that created them, speaks of an even higher "poetry of the stars":

> ...the poetry of the stars is in the silent meeting of soul with soul, at the confluence of the light and the dark, where the infinite prints its kiss on the forehead of the finite, where we can hear the music of the Great I AM peeling from the grand organ of creation through its countless reeds in endless harmony.

Tagore's words may give us a small idea of the extraordinary and ineffable inner experience of initiation, which is pointed to by Dylan in his song. Such an experience depends upon a deep surrender. Spiritual transformation begins with suffering and depends upon surrender. Again, Tagore:

> Our greatest hope is in this, that suffering is there. It is the language of imperfection. Its very utterance carries in it the trust in the perfect, like the baby's cry which would be dumb, if it had no faith in the mother. This suffering has driven man with his prayer knocking at the gate of the infinite in him, the divine, thus revealing his deepest instinct, his unreasoning faith in the reality of the ideal – the faith shown in the readiness for death, in the renunciation of all that belongs to the self ... It is the surrender of his self to be tuned for the music of the soul. This surrender is waited for, because the spiritual harmony cannot be effected except through freedom. Therefore man's willing surrender to the infinite is the commencement

of the union. Only then can God's love fully act upon man's soul through the medium of freedom.

So, "Señor (Tales of Yankee Power)" is a song of mystical surrender and initiation. It may not at first seem to be a specifically Christian initiation. However, that the prayer is addressed to "Señor," as the Spanish frequently address Christ, seems to suggest that it is Christian, as does the last stanza:

> Señor, señor, let's disconnect these cables
> Overturn these tables
> This place don't make sense to me no more
> Can you tell me what we're waiting for, señor?

After this initial crossing of the threshold, the fallen world makes no sense, and he is ready, with Christ, to start overturning tables. He is ready for apocalypse and wonders what we are waiting for.

But the esoteric depths of Dylan's mystical and initiatory experiences are revealed most strikingly in the last song on the *Street Legal* album, "Where Are You Tonight? (Journey Through Dark Heat)." This song begins with a reference to the "holy slow train," which here is called "a long-distance train," thus connecting this album, *Street Legal* with the next album *Slow Train Coming*, the first in his so-called born-again Christian period.

> There's a long-distance train rolling through the rain
> Tears on the letter I write
> There's a woman I long to touch and I miss her so much
> But she's drifting like a satellite

> There's a neon light ablaze in a green smoky haze
> Laughter down on Elizabeth Street
> And a lonesome bell tone in that valley of stone
> Where she bathed in a stream of pure heat
>
> Her father emphasized you got to be more than street-wise
> But he practiced what he preached from the heart
> A full-blooded Cherokee, he predicted to me
> The time and the place that the trouble would start

The "Slow Train" is a long-distance train moving through the "Hard Rain" confusions of our modern times. Slowly, one by one, the conversions happen, and gradually the effects of the conversions move out into the world through individuals. The inner experiences, which bring about those conversions, are moments in the life of those individuals, which as Emerson noted, are of such depth and intensity that we are constrained to ascribe more reality to them than to all other experience. The cultural historian, William Irwin Thompson, noted that such moments occur in the history of thought as well, and he aptly characterized such moments:

> ...there is a moment of freedom in which the containment of the ego of the individual and the culture is broken and the longer history of the soul is remembered. For a brief moment we have a sense of other possibilities; at a dramatic turning point on the road of history we come to a place where space-time curves and we can see

back to the beginning and forward to the transfiguration of the human race. But it is only a brief instant, for the road turns again, our vistas collapse, and we return to putting one foot in front of the other in the long march of human evolution.

When these moments pass, one returns to putting one foot in front of the other, but those moments remain in his memory, changing the nature of his reality. One longs for such moments, and lives for them. So there are tears on the letter he writes to "her," remembering (while hearing only a lonesome bell tone in the valley-like depths of his meditation that has a stillness and silence comparable to stone), that "she" was once there, bathed in pure heat. He recalls the advice of "her" father, that you have to be more than street-wise. That is, a merely pedantic or legalistic factuality is not sufficient for attaining truth. Full-blooded, native intelligence has revealed to him when and where the trouble would start, the trouble with the "dragon" referred to in "Señor." But around that meditative valley of stone, he is aware of the world "out there" as a place where "There's a neon light ablaze in a green smoky haze, laughter down on Elizabeth Street." Queen Elizabeth I, the illegitimate daughter of Henry VIII, gave her name to an age that is often thought of as one of material prosperity and artistic drabness, and in that sense, our contemporary world may be called "Elizabeth Street" with its "neon light" and its hollow laughter.

"Where Are You Tonight? (Journey Through Dark Heat)" is comprised of thirteen stanzas. The first three provide details of the background circumstances concerning the spiritual experience being remembered. Then comes stanza four, which has five lines instead of four and a different rhyme scheme, and represents a moment of peak intensity. This pattern repeats with stanzas eight and thirteen taking the same form and representing subsequent moments of peak intensity in this spiritual experience. In all three cases the leap in intensity calls upon the believing soul of the listener to follow. The first of these leaps is stanza four:

> There's a babe in the arms of a woman in a rage
> And a longtime golden-haired stripper onstage
> And she winds back the clock and she turns back the page
> Of a book that nobody can write
> Oh, where are you tonight?

The image contained in the first line can be readily understood as a poetic perception of the human self in the arms of Mother Nature who is in a rage over mankind's continued insensitivity. Behind Mother Nature we may wish to see also her own higher-self, the soul of the world or Sophia. The image of the next three lines is not so quickly understood, and one may need to come at this image from the context of the whole song after repeated exposure. In esotericism, an initiate may attain a degree of consciousness that permits him, as it is said, to read from the Akashic Record, or from what in the Bible is called the Book of Remembrances. This Akasha is a kind of cosmic memory in which all the events of time are preserved in eternity. This image in Dylan's song of "a longtime golden-haired stripper onstage" who can "wind back the clock" and "turn back the page/Of a book nobody can write" points to this esoteric dimension of visionary experience. From this peak we return to more details of this spiritual experience as they are remembered:

> The truth was obscure, too profound and too pure
> To live it you have to explode
> In that last hour of need, we entirely agreed
> Sacrifice was the code of the road
>
> I left town at dawn, with Marcel and St. John
> Strong men belittled by doubt
> I couldn't tell her what my private thoughts were
> But she had some way of finding them out
>
> He took dead-center aim but he missed just the same
> She was waiting, putting flowers on the shelf
> She could feel my despair as I climbed up her hair
> And discovered her invisible self

"Marcel," presumably Gabriel Marcel, is a contemporary French Christian thinker and writer, and St. John is the author of the fourth Gospel and of the last book of the New Testament, the visionary Revelations or Apocalypse. Dylan leaves town with them, that is, while meditating on their thoughts about the Christian mystery, he leaves or transcends ordinary consciousness. Although he could not tell "her" what his private thoughts were, "she" already knew what they were. With his will, "he" takes dead-center aim but misses just the same. One cannot get there by one's own will-power. But "she" was aware of his despair, and after the mystical climb up her "hair," an ascent of visionary perception, he finds "her" already there taking care of his spiritual home. In discovering "her" invisible self, he has in fact discovered his own true spiritual self.

This is much the same experience described in "Changing of the Guards," when he had followed "her down past the fountains where they lifted her veil." This is an experience beyond words. Compare the description given by the third century Neoplatonist, Plotinus:

> The difficulty is that awareness of the One comes not by knowing but by a Presence passing knowledge. In knowing, the mind takes account of things: it departs from unity and becomes lost in multiplicity. This other way lies beyond knowing. We urge you abandon discussion and heed the call of vision .... There the soul looks upon the fountains of Life and Spirit, the springs of Being, the well of Goodness, *the root of the soul*, These fountains flow eternally, without diminishment .... Now the man is merged in the Supreme, *molten*, into It, one with It. (Emphasis added)

Poised, so to speak, upon this inner peak, he has yet to make the final leap into the nirvanic reaches of being, into the very "root of the soul" itself. The intensity of this moment and this decision is expressed in the next stanza:

> There's a lion in the road, there's a demon escaped
> There's a million dreams gone, there's a landscape being raped
> As her beauty fades and I watch her undrape
> I won't, but then again, maybe I might
> Oh, if I could just find you tonight

In the depths of this experience, consciousness is so concentrated that it can no longer remain aware of the feminine complement, of the division of the inner being in the dynamic form of "male" and "female." The landscape being raped is the landscape of his own inner being as well as the outer landscape of nature, its outer reflection. At this peak of visionary experience they are one and the same. As he begins to dissolve into the nirvanic experience, she fades and unravels, so to speak. He thinks at first that he won't go on with it, but then again, maybe he might. Apparently he did, because now, back in the world putting one foot in front of the other and recalling it all, he cries out, "Oh, if I could just find you tonight." In the next set of circumstantial stanzas, the inner anguish and torment to be gone through in this deep experience is graphically related:

> I fought with my twin, that enemy within
> 'Til both of us fell by the way
> Horseplay and disease is killing me by degrees
> While the law looks the other way
>
> Your partners in crime hit me up for nickels and dimes
> The man you were lovin' could never get clean
> It felt outa place, my foot in his face
> But he should-a stayed where his money was green
>
> I bit into the root of forbidden fruit
> With the juice running down my leg
> Then I dealt with your boss, who'd never known about loss
> And who always was too proud to beg

The Journey Through Dark Heat

> There's a white diamond gloom on the dark
> side of this room
> And a pathway that leads up to the stars
> If you don't believe there's a price for this sweet
> paradise
> Remind me to show you the scars

The road to this paradise, to this supernal and numinous experience, is inwardly difficult, harder in fact than anything encountered in ordinary life, and he briefly and cogently recalls its difficulties: the fight with the enemy within against a backdrop of continual horseplay and disease. It's as if he had the joker side of our being in mind while speaking to himself here. A possible translation might go like this: "And you, you who continue to live under the lie, under the sign of the *Joker,* your partners always want to hit me up for small change, but the man you're loving, the "Joker-man" – he can *never* get clean. I had to get tough with him myself, with that joker side of myself, in order to get beyond him. I had to put my foot in his face, in the face of that satanic, luciferic force in the will that is too proud to beg, that keeps the ego from surrendering. I had to go the whole distance in confronting this dark power, which amounted to tasting the forbidden fruit by entering the deepest, darkest part of myself to face the reality of evil, and it was scary as hell and can only be had at a great price that leaves its scars."

The *Joker's* boss, Lucifer, is not used to losing, and his goal is to keep you proud like himself. But if you want to find out the truth, the truth that on the dark side of your being, within the white diamond gloom of inner-space, there really is a pathway that leads past the Gordian Knot of good and evil, that leads up to the stars, then you have to enter the turbulent space and make the journey through dark heat. However, there is a price to be paid, the price of earnest struggle and surrender. And if you don't believe there is such a price, he says, "just remind me to show you the scars."

"Come in," she had said long ago. But in going in so far he has reached the point of what amounts to biting into the "forbidden fruit" from the Tree of Life. There are two trees in paradise, and we have tasted but one, the Tree of Knowledge of Good and Evil:

> And the Lord God said, Behold, the man is become as one of us, to know good and evil: and now, lest he put forth his hand and take also of the tree of life, and eat, and live forever:
>
> Therefore, the Lord God sent him forth from the garden of Eden, to till the ground from whence he was taken.
>
> So he drove out the man; and he placed at the east of the garden of Eden Cherubims, and a flaming sword which turned every way, to keep the way of the tree of life.

With our knowledge of good and evil we are east of Eden and the Tree of Life is protected by the *flaming* sword of the Cherubim, and its forbidden fruit along with it. From the Fall it is the forbidden fruit, but not for all time. In the *Apocalypse* or *Revelations* of St. John, the Risen Christ says,

> He that overcometh will I give to eat of the tree of life, which is in the midst of the paradises of God.

To eat of the Tree of Life is the reward of eternal life given by Christ, which is to say by Christ-consciousness, which alone can reveal the mystery upon which life is founded. It is given to those who "overcome." As the Tree of Knowledge is the outer aspect of the Tree, so is the Tree of Life the inner aspect. The Tree of Knowledge is in the center of the World, but the Tree of Life is the center of the center, within "the paradises of God." Overcoming the world is a journey through the dark heat of the Cherubim's flaming sword, and involves a mystical death in Christ. Small wonder that Dylan could sing with the power of conviction on the *Saved* album, "Are you ready, I hope you're ready." (Mr. Jones, it would seem that something is indeed happening here, and it is *still* happening. Maybe it's high time we found out what it is).

In this journey through dark heat, in this experience of being "molten into It," as Plotinus put it, *She* is necessarily lost, not in the sense of division or separation, but in the sense of incorporation or absorption. As he returns to the everyday world, putting one foot in front of the other and remembering that divine experience, he is aware, once again, of being without her.

> There's a new day at dawn and I've finally arrived
> If I'm there in the morning, baby, you'll know I've survived
> I can't believe it, I can't believe I'm alive
> But without you it just doesn't seem right
> Oh, where are you tonight?

A new day is beginning to dawn. After this journey through dark heat he cannot doubt that. The "Slow Train" is winding its way through the tail end of night. When the morning does finally arrive, when the lights go up, if he is still alive in the body, then she will know that he has survived his long vigil under the night sky of earthbound consciousness. But now he *knows*, and he knows that he knows: he has eaten of the Tree of Life, and the joy is so great that it is hard to believe he could still actually be alive in a physical body. And until "she" is with him always – not just in moments – it won't seem quite right. "Oh, where are you tonight."

All the songs on the *Street Legal* album pertain to deeply esoteric spiritual experiences on the threshold. And it seems significant to me that Dylan rushed this album into production in order to release it prior to *Slow Train Coming*, the album that brought a flood of negative reaction to his expression of Christian consciousness. The Christian lyrics of his so-called "born-again" period could only have been misconstrued as a form of naive fundamentalism, or conventional Christianity, if the *Street Legal* album were either ignored or deeply misunderstood, which was the case for many in his audience.

10

FAR FROM THE TURBULENT SPACE

> In how many churches, by how many prophets, tell me, is man made sensible that he is an infinite soul; that the earth and heavens are passing into his mind; that he is drinking forever the soul of God?
>
> -Emerson

Slow Train Coming is musically one of Dylan's finest albums. At a time when many Christian fundamentalists held the conviction that rock and roll itself was diabolical, that it was an instrument of the devil corrupting the souls of the young with deviously hidden, subliminal messages, Dylan produced an album that combined unquestionably splendid rock and roll music with lyrics that plainly and powerfully expressed Christian sentiments that even fervent fundamentalists could identify with. This album, from its first song, "Gotta Serve Somebody," to its last, "When He Returns," is the work of a man who is earnestly and livingly aware of Christ as a real Presence working mysteriously in the Hard Rain confusions of modern times.

Out of this awareness Dylan has been able to make a number of sharply critical observations about our spiritually decadent culture and civilization that are agreeable even to ardent fundamentalists. However, Dylan's Christianity is the culmination of a deeply mystical and artistic quest, which has led him into the esoteric dimensions of being. The authority and power of his lyrics derive from that personal quest and not from beliefs that are held as mere hand-me-down dogmas. His so-called Christian lyrics are as much the expression of the inner man as his earlier and later songs, and are of a piece with them.

The Hard Rain confusions of the 20th century, which have continued unabated into the 21st, are a veritable Gordian's Knot, which promises to confound even the elect. On the one hand, there exists the pervasive assumption that scientific thought has somehow finally put to rest all the superstitions of antiquated religious belief. On the other hand, institutional religions continue to offer their flocks time-worn formulas that nevertheless appear helpless to reveal the living springs from which those formulas arose. Interwoven with this there is also the frantic re-emergence of every spiritual movement and cult known to history, together with a host of zany and apparently new ones. All the while the long rope of runaway technology threatens to hang us all. This overwhelming confusion in the spiritual life of modern man is what Dylan often refers to as the "flood," as in the song, "Down in the Flood":

> Well, it' sugar for sugar
> And salt for salt
> If you go down in the flood
> It's gonna be your own fault

The positive side of this mad spiritual confusion is that we are necessarily and unequivocally thrown back on ourselves. Those sincerely seeking the truth of the mystery of life can now do no other than "go in" to find the truth out for themselves, and out of themselves. Failing this, "If you go down in the flood/It's gonna be your fault."

Dylan's personal and artistic quest led him to a deep mystical experience of Christ-consciousness, and that seemed to trouble a large segment of his fans. But they apparently had failed to recognize the genuine esoteric dimension of Dylan's quest and mistook his Christianity as synonymous with a decadent form of institutional religion. They found it difficult to understand how Dylan could sing a song like "I Believe in You" with unwavering conviction:

> They ask me how I feel
> And if my love is real
> And how I know I'll make it through
> And they, they look at me and frown
> They'd like to drive me from this town
> They don't want me around
> 'Cause I believe in you.

Dylan has remained largely misunderstood, right from the beginning of his career. In light of this fact, one marvels that he nevertheless became so rich and famous. One begins to sense behind his charisma, behind his talents and his *charisms*, the mysterious working of a more-than-human power. When one steps back from the study of these lyrics to consider in a panoramic view the whole career of this man, one cannot help but have a sober respect for Dylan's dedication to his art in the face of unconscionable miscomprehension. His artistic journey through the world was and remains a personal and private affair, for himself and for his friends. For only they can share fully in such a private prayerful hymn as "I Believe in You":

> Don't let me drift too far,
> Keep me where you are
> Where I will always be renewed.
> And that which you've given me today
> Is worth more than I can pay
> And no matter what they say
> I believe in you.

For Dylan's friends, even his Christian lyrics incorporate riddles which, when they are penetrated, reveal the authenticity of his esoteric experience. The uniform quality of those riddles provides the *signet* and seal of personal truthfulness that justifies his right to utter his testimony. For example, the initial inner perception with which this book began, of man's division into the *Joker* and the *Thief*, finds its natural extension in the lyrics of "Pressing On":

> Many try to stop me, shake me up in my mind
> They say, "Prove to me that He is Lord, show me a sign"
> What kind of sign they need when it all comes from within
> When what's lost has been found, what's to come has already been?

"What's to come," what is always coming, is *death*. But when you find what has been lost, which is to say, the truth of your own spiritual being inwardly united with the eternal, then death, which is really only the death of the moon-ego, has already happened. It all comes from within. You have to find that out for yourself, and out of yourself. As you strengthen the things that remain of your own spiritual being, you will be guided gradually into the depths of spiritual reality. Once you make the commitment to press on, nothing can hold you back:

> Shake the dust off your feet, don't look back
> Nothing now can hold you down, nothing that you lack
> Temptation's not an easy thing, Adam given the devil reign
> Because he sinned I got no choice, it run in my vein

Adam, the First Adam, who is the spiritual being of Mankind, sinned. Of course, he had to sin, he had to find out about good *and* evil in order to mature as a spiritual being. The Fall is a cosmic, livingly mythological drama of the evolution of men as individual spirits. In biting into the Apple, he fell from grace, from the self-sustaining harmony of heaven, and lost – though only temporarily – his true spiritual identity. When Christ entered into earth evolution as a *mystical fact*, he became as St. Paul perceived, the New Adam, the new spiritual being of Mankind. But the First Adam is still there in our veins as a force of nature to be surmounted and overcome. The way to overcome it is to unite ourselves with the New Adam, to die in Christ. But to do this, like giving ear to the *Thief* in "All Along The Watchtower," is not a decision one can make abstractly or intellectually. Words are cheap and intentions are futile. Dying in Christ is the journey inward through the turbulent space of your own being to confront your own unknown self. Only through the suffering and the surrender involved in this experience, worked out within the privacy of prayerful introspection, can one come to that deep emotion of repentance, which Dylan expressed in "Saving Grace":

> If you find it in Your Heart, can I be forgiven?
> Guess I owe You some kind of apology
> I've escaped death so many times, I know I'm only living
> By the saving grace that's over me
>
> By this time I'd-a thought I would be sleeping
> In a pine box for all eternity
> My faith keeps me alive, but I still be weeping
> For the saving grace that's over me

It is easy to see how these two stanzas might be construed as routine simulations of conventional Christian cant. But the three remaining stanzas of this song each contain a riddle of their own, indicative of the personal living experience behind it.

> Well, the death of life, then comes the resurrection
> Wherever I am welcome is where I'll be
> I put all my confidence in Him, my sole protection
> Is the saving grace that's over me

Yes, quite matter-of-factly, after this "death of life," the death of the moon-ego, comes the resurrection. Once that has happened, you are beyond not only the letter of the law but also beyond the restrictive peer-group pressure of sectarian opinion. Now, like Christ, you many even find yourself consorting with publicans and sinners – if that's where you find yourself welcome. Living with the consciousness that He is your sole protection, what others may happen to *think* matters not at all.

> Well, the devil's shining light, it can be most blinding
> But to search for love, that ain't nothing more than vanity
> As I look around this world all that I'm finding
> Is the saving grade that's over me

This is quite a telling little riddle and deserves our considered attention. If you have come so far as to see for yourself, and out of yourself – in the sense of gnosis – that He is your sole protection, then the search for love (or wealth or renown or whatever, and all the nervous making-haste for them), is no more than the vain thought that *you*, in and of yourself, can make them happen. Christ knows your needs even before you ask, and these things are all finally in His hands even if His wisdom sometimes appears foolish to men. Confirmed by the journey through dark heat, one sees in the world wherever one looks, the hidden working of the saving grace over us all.

> The wicked know no peace and you just can't fake it
> There's only one road and it leads to Calvary
> It gets discouraging at times, but I know I'll make it
> By the saving grace that's over me

There is only one road, and it leads to Calvary: to crucifixion, death and resurrection. The important thing is not to put a name on this road and call it Christian, but to make the journey inward yourself. Discover for yourself whether this is true or not, that there is only one road. Then, after you have gone the distance and know it out of your own experience, as *gnosis*, then call it by whatever name you wish. Christ by any other name is still Christ.

The authenticity of this experience exists, and though many religious denominations preach to some extent the formula for it, most fail when it comes to translating it into living terms that could actually guide someone to it. Sad to say, even many of the clergy, for all their good intentions and deeds, have not gone the distance and some of them suffer from a form of near-sightedness, if not outright blindness. By a kind of perverse magic, those religious leaders become unconsciously the blind who are leading the blind. The name of Christ has become a kind of golden watch dangled before the "dark eyes" of the sheep, sometimes by well-meaning but incompetent pastors and sometimes by unscrupulous preachers intent on preying upon the deeply sacred but unconscious needs and yearnings of their followers. The inner longing for truth is there in each soul, but the path is full of snares. Too much of what calls itself Christianity today — to the extent it keeps you by means of hollow rituals and dead dogmas from entering the "turbulent space" of your own inner being — only adds to the spiritual confusion of modern life.

There are many today who are able to see through the charades that frequently characterize many of the churches, sects and cults that surround us. Unfortunately, however, only a few are able to see all the way through to the real possibility of authentic experience. Many of those who are critical of religion in a general way but have not gone the distance themselves, tend to affect a sort of superior attitude toward religion, and with a condescending manner would dismiss the whole matter. On the other hand, those blindly following the blind fail to enter the "turbulent space" because of the lifeless and impotent guidance they have received from their religious leaders. Such leaders too often balk at entering the "turbulent space" themselves, due to an unconscious fear disguised as a sort of pious vanity. In "Property of Jesus" Dylan sang:

> You can laugh at salvation, you can play Olympic games
> You think that when you rest at last you'll go back from where you came
> But you've picked up quite a story and you've changed since the womb
> What happened to the real you, you've been captured but by whom?

Somewhere between birth and the present, the real you has been lost, captured by a story, a lie and by the prince of lies. You can laugh at salvation, but it won't change the deep reality of what is. There is only one road, the road into and through the "turbulent space." The one who will not do this remains a "dead man" in the spiritual sense, taking life as a joke. Dylan, on his next album, addresses this spiritual ghost or specter in "Dead Man, Dead Man":

> Uttering idle words from a reprobate mind
> Clinging to strange promises, dying on the vine
> Never bein' able to separate the good from the bad
> Ooh, who can stand it, I can't stand it
> It's makin' me feel so sad
>
> Dead man, dead man
> When will you arise?
> Cobwebs in your mind
> Dust upon your eyes

In the next stanza Dylan discerns the intimate connection between faith and love, and can recognize the "dead man" even by the arrogant tilt of this head:

> Satan got you by the heel, there's a bird's nest in your hair
> Do you have any faith at all? Do you have any love to share?
> The way that you hold your head, cursin' God with every move
> Ooh who can stand it, I can't stand it
> What are you trying' to prove?

In this song, the "Dead Man" is more of a generic term pointing to the mass of mankind who are still under the sign of the *Joker*, rather than a designation for an individual. Later, Dylan would see him on a larger, almost mythical scale as the "Jokerman." Whereas the *Joker* is specifically an element within our individual psychological make-up that keeps us turned to the world and prevents us from "going in," the "Jokerman" is a personification or image of the cosmic being who incarnates in Mankind via the *Joker* element in each individual consciousness. Not the phantasm of worn-out Christian mythology, but a real force actively present and perceptible to one who has gone into and through the "turbulent space." This is the enemy Dylan aims at in "Shot of Love" when he sings:

> Why would I want to take your life?
> You've only murdered my father, raped his wife
> Tattooed my babies with a poison pen
> Mocked my God, humiliated my friends

The "Jokerman," as the adversary force in the world, has murdered the Spirit; raped Nature; tattooed his lovingly rendered artistic creations with the poison pen of uncomprehending criticism; mocked his personal God; and humiliated his friends. But the "Jokerman," as the satanic adversarial power, also shows his face through the *Joker* element in each individual human being. Because of this dual aspect, "Jokerman" as a cosmic spiritual force and "Jokerman" as he manifests in individuals, the song "Jokerman" contains a certain ambiguity. For the poet's vision is focused now on the cosmic aspect, now on the individual. The first stanza begins with a view of the Jokerman seen through the window of the human individual:

> Standing on the waters casting your bread
> While the eyes of the idol with the iron head are glowing
> Distant ships sailing into the mist
> You were born with a snake in both of your fists
> while a hurricane was blowing
> Freedom just around the corner for you
> But with the truth so far off, what good will it do?

These are sharply chiseled images with esoteric connotations. The "you" of the song is the human individual standing on the "waters" of his conscious being, throwing the "bread" of his life away while the dead eyes of the idol of materialism glow. The "distant ships," which are sailing into the "mist" of this scene from parts unknown, remind one of Dylan's 1963 song, "When the Ship Comes In." Here are the last two stanzas from that early song:

> Oh the foes will rise
> With sleep still in their eyes

> And they'll jerk from their beds and think they're dreamin'
> But they'll pinch themselves and squeal
> And know that it's for real
> The hour when the ship comes in
>
> Then they'll raise their hands
> Sayin' we'll meet all your demands
> But we'll shout from the bow your days are numbered.
> And like Pharaoh's tribe
> They'll be drownded in the tide
> And like Goliath, they'll be conquered

These "distant ships," with their cargo of spiritual power and consciousness, begin to be distinguishable from the mist as they return upon the scene. At the same time, the Jokerman, as a human individual, is born with a "snake" in both his fists. This is an esoterically loaded image. The snake represents the basis of the "ego" in the same way that the horse represents the basis of the human intelligence per se. Also, esotericists will tell you that in bringing our hands together so that the right and left sides of our being meet in the sense of touch, the fundamental experience of egoity arises. This is why we bring our hands together in prayer. The hurricane that is blowing in this scene, as a spiritual perception, represents the Hard Rain spiritual confusions of modern times.

The tragic element of this picture, though, is that the Jokerman, as the individual human being, has lost his ancient connection to spiritual reality and has not yet awakened to the fact that distant ships are now coming into view. So he is wasting away his life in the dark satanic mills of materialistic, technological madness. Although the distant ships are coming slowly into the mist of this madness, although the "holy slow train" is coming up around the bend, he is about to go down in the flood. The tragedy is that freedom is just around the corner for him, for this man who is still under the sign of the *Joker* (and, as such, is a living embodiment of the "Jokerman"), yet he does not see it. And because he cannot see it, the refrain paints a picture of his precarious and primarily unconscious circumstance in life:

> Jokerman dance to the nightingale tune
> Bird fly high by the light of the moon
> Oh, oh, oh, Jokerman

The Jokerman's life, even if he doesn't know it, is a life lived out within the mystery upon which life itself is founded: the nightingale tune. The bird of his soul flies high, though that flight is not in the light of the spiritual sun. Rather, it is in the "lunar," or lunatic light that dominates the night sky of earth-bound consciousness, the light of the moon-ego. The last line is like an interjection expressing the wonder of it: Oh, Jokerman, when will you see it, when will you wake up. This portrait of the individual as an embodiment of the Jokerman continues in the next stanza:

> So swiftly the sun sets in the sky
> You rise up and say goodbye to no one
> Fools rush in where angels fear to tread
> Both of their futures, so full of dread, you don't show one
> Shedding off one more layer of skin
> Keeping one step ahead of the persecutor within

Life for the *Joker* will end quickly enough. Seventy, eighty or even a hundred years — but if that's all there is, it is nothing in the vast expanses of time. When the "sun in the sky" sets, when death comes, there will be no one for the Joker to say goodbye to. Fools and angels go together into the mystery: fools rushing headlong, angels with fear and trembling. And even if their mysterious future seems so full of dread, at least they have one. But the Jokerman, who keeps ahead of the *Thief*, that persecutor within, has no future at all. In the next stanza, we get the "Jokerman" in his majestically sinister proportions:

> You're a man of the mountains, you can walk on the clouds
> Manipulator of crowds, you're a dream twister
> You're going to Sodom and Gomorrah
> But what do you care? Ain't nobody there would want to marry your sister
> Friend to the martyr, a friend to the woman of shame
> You look into the fiery furnace, see the rich man without any name

The prince of this world, the manipulator of crowds and the dream twister, is headed for destruction. But he doesn't care, because his "sister," his consciousness, is the spiritual complement of nothing. He is a friend to the martyr in the ironic sense that he is the force that makes martyrdom necessary, but he is really only a friend to the woman of shame, to Babylon, who is the mother of lies. The adversarial spirit, this "Jokerman," is quite capable of looking into the fiery furnace of creation, into the mystery of creation, where he can see that spiritually rich man who in eternity has no name. In 1968 Dylan said in an interview in response to a question about his having taken the name Bob Dylan, that, "Names are labels so we can refer to one another. But deep inside us we don't have a name. We have no name." This is much the same perception that the French poet, Paul Valery, expressed in his essay, "Man And The Sea Shell":

> The problem after all is no more futile nor any more naive than speculation about *who made* a certain fine work in music or poetry; whether it was born of the Muse, or sent by Fortune, or whether it was the fruit of long labor. To say that someone composed it, that his name was Mozart or Virgil, is not to say much; a statement of this sort is lifeless, *for the creative spirit in us bears no name*; such a remark merely eliminates from our concern all men but one, within whose inner mystery the enigma lies hidden, intact .... (Emphasis added)

When the "Jokerman" looks into the fiery furnace, he beholds his enemy: that nameless one, the creative spirit, who alone overcomes.

> Well, the Book of Leviticus and Deuteronomy
> The law of the jungle and the sea are your only teachers
> In the smoke of the twilight on a milk-white steed
> Michelangelo indeed could have carved out your features
> Resting in the fields, far from the turbulent space
> Half asleep near the stars with a small dog licking your face

In this stanza the "Jokerman" is pictured in both his aspects, one superimposed upon the other. The Jokerman, as individual, has for his teachers the law of the jungle, the law of the sea, and the dusty ancient books. But these are his "only" teachers because he refuses to go into that "turbulent space" in order to find out for himself, and out of himself. The hordes of human individuals still living under the sign of the *Joker* give life thereby to the monumental phantasm of the "Jokerman," whose proportions are indeed now gargantuan. If he were the god he would have us take him for, it would take an artist of Michelangelo's rank to carve out his features: a huge figure astride a milk-white steed. But Dylan captures his true essence through the picture of the Jokerman, as he comes to life in the individual, resting in the field *far from the turbulent space*, with a small dog, the moon-ego, licking his face.

> Well, the rifleman's stalking the sick and the lame
> Preacherman seeks the same, who'll get there first is uncertain
> Nightsticks and watercannons, teargas, padlocks
> Molotov cocktails and rocks behind every curtain
> False-hearted judges dying in the webs that they spin
> Only a matter of time 'til night comes steppin' in

The rifleman and the preacherman are both representations of the Joker-man. The one seeks power over the body by force and the other seeks power over the mind by persuasion, and the target they both zero in on like vultures is the spiritually blind and lame. Then, Dylan bombards us with a rapid collage of images that suggests the oppressions of a police-state. But the violence in the world is a projection of what lives in the heart of man (behind every curtain). These are all aspects of the dominance of the "Jokerman" in our world, which produces the Hard Rain confusions of our day. And those still under the sign of the *Joker* are dying in the webs they spin. Yet, it's only a matter of time, both for the *Joker* and for the "Jokerman."

> It's a shadowy world, skies are slippery grey
> A woman just gave birth to a prince today and dressed him in scarlet
> He'll put the priest in his pocket, put the blade to the heat
> Take the motherless children off the street and place them at the feet of a harlot
> Oh, Jokerman, you know what he wants
> But, Jokerman, you don't show any response

This is the picture of a seemingly never-ending story, a never-ending tragedy. A woman gives birth to a prince. All are born as princes to begin with, or rather, all were born to *become* kings. But at birth, we are "dressed in scarlet," in the body of desire that burns in the blood. Then as we grow, we reenact the Fall within ourselves. Eventually, as the ego waxes, religion (the priest) becomes something merely handy that we can keep in our pocket and make use of for egotistic purposes. And so, under the lie of the moon-ego, we unconsciously prepare for the ancient ritual (put the blade to the heat) of the slaughter of the innocents. Spiritually blind, the *Joker* unknowingly adds his life to the power of the prince of this world, whose aim is to capture all who are born of woman.

The *Joker*, as one of those who are unaware of Sophia, is a "motherless child," and by living the Jokerman-lie, he unwittingly perpetuates the slaughter of innocents. Newborns growing up under his influence will learn the lie from him, and will in this way wind up being placed at the feet of a harlot: Babylon, the mother of lies. The new generation will continue as a new wave of orphans, as "motherless children," who are unaware of their spiritual origins. The "Jokerman," the prince of this world, knows well what the soul wants and is looking for when it enters life in the world. But from him the soul never receives a response concerning that deep need.

When rightly understood this lyric is a work of art that concentrates an astounding degree of spiritual perception. Upon hearing the recording, it is a thing of beauty. As the first song of Dylan's *after* his so-called Christian phase, it confirms that the essential nature of his spiritual vision has not altered in the least. If one studies Dylan's work closely enough, one comes gradually to the ironic conclusion that this "mercurial artist" – of whom it has been said: he changes persona every few years – has really remained steady as a rock.

11

WHERE THE SWIFT DON'T WIN THE RACE

> In nature we are blind and lame like a child before its birth. But in the spiritual life we are born in freedom. And then because we are freed from the blind bondage of nature she is illuminated to us, and where we saw before mere envelopment we now see the mother.
>
> -Tagore

On the same album with "Jokerman" there is a song called "I and I." The stanzas of this song revolve around the riddle-like refrain as if upon a pivot. The quiet, personal theme of this song unfolds in unostentatious images which nevertheless touch upon the major elements of Dylan's vision, even going surreptitiously into the heart of the mystery. We meet a "strange woman" in the first stanza, and if we have accustomed ourselves to Dylan's eccentric manner of expressing himself, we can recognize that she is an image of his soul-bride. She is perceived as a "strange" woman now only because of the newer and deeper insights she has recently brought to him, insights that have produced in him a profound sense of serenity.

> Been so long since a strange woman has slept in my bed
> Look how sweet she sleeps, how free must be her dreams
> In another lifetime she must have owned the world, or been faithfully wed
> To some righteous king who wrote psalms beside moonlit streams
>
> I and I
> In creation where one's nature neither honors nor forgives
> I and I
> One says to the other, no man sees my face and lives

It seems a long while since Psyche has come into his "bed" in a form of consciousness that could bring him strangely new and refreshing inspirations. He gazes upon her as she sleeps, in awe of her beautiful dreams of freedom, and tenderly, lovingly – in all humility – he recognizes that she is a soul-bride worthy of a righteous king who writes psalms beside moonlit streams. Then, the refrain comes in like a harsh flash of memory reminding him of the fallen state in which no man can see the face of God without first dying. This spurs him to the realization that as wonderful as this solemn peace is, one cannot rest here indefinitely. One must continuously change or pay more for remaining the same. It is time to move on:

> Think I'll go out for a walk
> Not much happenin' here, nothin' ever does
> Besides, if she wakes up now, she'll just want me to talk
> I got nothin' to say, 'specially about whatever was

If she wakes up now, she will want him to talk, to create, to express himself in light of her new inspirations. In these calm moments of inner repose, nothing much ever happens. But "permanent bliss" is an illusion, and even on the inner planes the endless journey continues. Again, the refrain comes in like a jab, urging him beyond whatever *was*. As always, before lighting out for new unknown territory, there comes a brief recapitulation of what has led up to this sacred moment of transition:

> Took an untrodden path once, where the swift don't win the race
> It goes to the worthy, who can divide the word of truth
> Took a stranger to teach me, to look into justice's beautiful face
> And to see an eye for an eye and a tooth for a tooth

Dylan, like Robert Frost, has taken a road "less traveled by," one which has truly made all the difference in the world. Speed, swiftness, cleverness – these mean nothing here on this path. This path is for the worthy, those who have *earned it*, not the new way or the old-fashioned way but the real way, the only way there is: by dividing the word of truth, realizing it is a sword that cuts both ways. It took a "stranger" once, perhaps like the "strange woman" he has just left, to teach him to look into justice's beautiful face where the eye for eye and tooth for tooth show plainly that "we are what we see." The next stanza then refers to the "holy slow train":

> Outside of two men on a train platform there's nobody in sight
> They're waiting for spring to come, smoking down the track
> The world could come to an end tonight, but that's all right
> She should still be there sleepin' when I get back

There are two men waiting for the "holy slow train," waiting for the springtime, the Easter of evolution, to come smoking down the track. There is nobody else in sight because this is one of those lonely peaks attained by "yankee power." There are *two* men waiting, and they are both the "I" of this song. One is the ordinary physical man, and the other is the inner spiritual man. What is born of the flesh is flesh, and what is born of the spirit is spirit. At death, the flesh will die, but not the spirit. Because Dylan has gone into and through the "turbulent space," his "I" has been reborn from flesh to spirit, but the physical man, who has already died metaphorically, has not yet died physically. If he does, if the world comes to an end tonight, that's all right, because he *knows* that she will be there – in the spirit – waiting for him.

In the rebirth of the "I" from the man of flesh to the man of spirit, the "I" of the individual is born through freedom into harmony with the Great I-AM. As Tagore wrote:

> The ultimate end of freedom is also to know that "I am." But it is the liberation of man's

consciousness from separateness of self into unity with all. This freedom is not perfect in its mere extension, but its true perfection is in its intensity, which is love.

Living with the consciousness of being two men, one of flesh, one of spirit, precipitates an excruciatingly trying polarity. The difficulties of this extremely tense and active inner life are sketched in the next stanza.

> Noontime, and I'm still pushin' myself along the road, the darkest part
> Into the narrow lanes, I can't stumble or stay put
> Someone else is speakin' with my mouth, but I'm listening only to my heart
> I've made shoes for everyone, even you, while I still go barefoot

It is noontime for the man of flesh but for the man of spirit who is pushing himself along the road, it is the *darkest part*. Here, he is making his way into the darkest part of the mystery of life: the mystery of the "I." Here, at the heights, in the narrow lanes of the mystery, he doesn't dare stumble or stop. He must go on with the change or pay more dearly for remaining the same.

It is strange to have the experience that when you speak, it's as if someone else were speaking through you. When the man of flesh is turned over to the "Great I-AM," the I that is now the I of the spiritual man, has to concentrate without distraction upon listening only to his heart in order for the power of the Holy Spirit to be able to work through his mouth without contamination. If the I of the spiritual man fails to do so, egoistic elements may slip into the utterance, falsifying it. This has to do with the paradoxical injunction: "let not thy left hand know what thy right hand doeth."

Here is the darkest part of the road. Even in this moment of darkness, while his mouth is being used by the Spirit for its purpose, he is listening to his heart and can hear it telling *him* that even though he, "Bob Dylan," has made shoes for everyone ('shoes' being inspirational aid), even for Robert Allen Zimmerman, the man of flesh, now (as he realizes) the "I" as the spiritual man still goes naked and alone as a metaphysically naked "I am." In the darkest part, one goes naked and barefoot, existentially vulnerable, through the final veil of the mystery.

In a book by Rudolf Steiner called *Eleven European Mystics* (also titled: *Mysticism At The Dawn of The Modern Age*), light is thrown on this mystery of the I from many sides through a study of such mystics as Meister Eckhart, Nicolas of Cusa, Jacob Boehme, Angelus Silesius and others. Steiner wrote:

> The understanding of the suspension of what is individual in the personality, of the I in favor of the All-I, is regarded by deeper natures as the secret revealing itself within man, as the primordial mystery of life. For this too Goethe has found an apt expression: "And so long as you do not have it, this Die and Become, you are only a dreary guest on the dark earth."

Meister Eckhart wrote, "Foolish people deem that they should look upon God as though He stood there and they here. It is not thus. God and I are one in the act of knowing." He also said, "The eye by which I see God is the same eye with which God sees me. My eye and God's eye is one eye and one seeing and one knowing and one feeling." My eye and God's eye is one eye. In a sense, that eye is the "I" that has known "this Die and Become." This is not to say that the individual is God, but because the individual freely surrenders his selfhood, the All-I, or the Great I-AM, enters into him.

Steiner, in his penetrating study of these mystics, speaks knowingly of this mystical transformation, "Thus the soul must look into itself; there it will find its I, its selfhood. If it stops at this, it separates itself from the complete." It is a matter of "the overcoming of selfhood through selfhood itself." He then goes on to say:

> It is in his self that the highest light shines for man. But this light only gives the right reflection to his world of ideas when man is aware that it is not the light of his self, but the universal light of the world. Therefore there is no more important knowledge than self-knowledge; and at the same time there is none which so completely leads beyond itself. When the "self" knows itself aright it is already no longer a "self."

This is the "primordial mystery of life," the mystery of the I in which one comes to understand the meaning of Christ's words, "He that findeth his life shall lose it: and he that loseth his life for my sake shall find it." Dylan indicated already in 1965 that he was concerned with this mystery in the surrealistic, free verse liner notes he wrote for the *Highway 61 Revisited* album:

> you are right john cohen – quazimodo was right – mozart was right – I cannot say the word eye anymore...when I speak this word

> eye, it is as if I am speaking of somebody's eye that I faintly remember...there is no eye – there is only a series of mouths – long live the mouths – your rooftop – if you don't already know – has been demolished...eye is plasma & you are right about that too – you are lucky – you don't have to think about such things as eyes & rooftops & quazimodo.

In "I and I" when he pushes himself along in the narrow lanes, it is the darkest part of the road where the light of the self goes out in order that a greater light might shine. Consider Meister Eckhart's words, "For everything the understanding can grasp, and everything desire demands, is not God. Where understanding and desire have an end, *there it is dark*, there does God shine. There that power unfolds in the soul which is wider than the wide heavens." (Emphasis added)

In 1975 Dylan, along with Jacques Levy, wrote an extraordinary song called "Black Diamond Bay." It was never a popular song, but it is certainly a masterpiece of its kind. In it, the art of poetry is merged with the story-telling art of the balladeer to reveal the depths of mysticism involved in the mystery of the I. From a literary standpoint, it is an epic in miniature.

"Black Diamond Bay" is a story twice-told, and in being retold, tells another, larger tale. We get the story of Black Diamond Bay initially in the first six stanzas. In this first telling, we live through the tragedy of Black Diamond Bay as if the song were a movie or a novel. Indeed, it is a third-person rendering of complex characters in a crisis. Then, in the last stanza, the whole event is reduced to a mere news item in the life of a suddenly first-person narrator who lives, not at Black Diamond Bay, but somewhere else. This radical shift in the song produces an effect similar to the experience of waking up from a dream. First we experience the disaster that occurs on Black Diamond Bay in sharp, moving details, and then we wake up somewhere else, safely first-person and unconcerned.

On the ground level, "Black Diamond Bay" tells of the destruction by volcano of an island and portrays the desperation of the characters on that island. In the first six stanzas we identify with the characters naturally enough, but then we are led suddenly to switch our identification to the "I" of the last stanza, who seems little concerned about the tragedy. On this level we may be tempted to think that the song merely wishes to describe a deplorable tendency found often enough in modern man, the disinclination to get involved with the suffering of his contemporaries. But Black Diamond Bay is a place to which the "I" of the last stanza "never did plan to go anyway." For him, it is a place as unreal as last night's dreams.

On another level, "Black Diamond Bay" is an intricate portrayal of the "Hard Rain" confusions of modern times that are pandemic and which are bound to end in catastrophe. This Hard Rain confusion stems from modern man's failure to attain to Wisdom or Sophia, who is here, center-stage. However, modern man has failed in his relationship with her, and the portrayal of that failure is told in this story with consummate skill.

Before we get into the song, however, let's consider some of the ironies embedded in this masterpiece. Black Diamond Bay is not a bay at all, but an island. And black diamonds are not diamonds, but merely coal, which is carbon that has yet to undergo the transformations that can turn it into diamonds. Is Black Diamond Bay then a harbor full of deposits waiting to be transformed, an island mine?

The "hard luck story that you're gonna hear" happens in a gambling house on an island that resembles a playground resort for wealthy tourists. The characters, in their order of appearance, are: an unnamed woman, the Greek, the desk clerk, a soldier, a tiny man, the dealer, the loser, and a stranger. On the symbolic level, like a good mystery play, the characters are themselves symbols. They constitute a kind of symbolic writing for telling this story. And the story they tell is the story of the modern soul.

The island, Black Diamond Bay, represents at the same time the self that has not yet been reborn or regenerated and the world, as its unconscious projection, the world of ordinary reality. The gambling house is a picture both of the individual consciousness in its fallen state by which one places his bets, decides what to and what not to believe; it is also the fallen world as the scene of this gambling activity. All of the characters, except for the woman, picture forth parts of or forces within the unregenerated soul. She pictures forth the ineffable spiritual essence of the soul itself. This unnamed woman is the soul, but not merely the soul of an individual. She is also Wisdom, who is the supersensible life of the soul itself. Spiritually all things are one. The soul of an individual, in its sublime existence, is inwardly in living connection to the great Wisdom that informs the natural world. In short, "She" pictures forth that part of our being most precious to us, and at the same time, that Divinity who holds all of creation, including ourselves, in its embrace. She is the actual living Beauty that is the Mind of God. The poet begins with a portrait of her in the initial seven lines of the first stanza:

> Up on the white veranda
> She wears a necktie and a Panama hat
> Her passport shows a face
> From another time and place
> She looks nothin' like that

> And all the remnants of her recent past
> Are scattered in the wild wind

Although veranda means porch, its original meaning is balcony, and she appears "up on" the white veranda. The word necktie suggests that her connection to us is at the neck, the throat, that is, through speech, through the word. The word Panama, as Pan-ama, can suggest "All-soul." The photograph on her passport, which is our memory of her, both literary and folk memory, shows that when she was around in earlier times, she looked quite different. But then, all the remnants of her presence here in the recent past have long since been scattered in the wild wind of the spiritual confusions of the present day. In the final lines of the stanza, we are shown the situation of the soul in relation to the fallen world, which is destined for sure destruction.

> She walks across the marble floor
> Where a voice from the gambling room is calling her to come on in
> She smiles, walks the other way
> As the last ship sails and the moon fades away
> From Black Diamond Bay.

She smiles and walks the other way because she does not obey the commands of the ego. She walks serenely on the "marble floor" but we, as egos, are down here in the fallen world where, cut off from consciousness of the spiritual world, we are constrained to guess about what is real, and to place our bets. What Lady Luck is to superstition, she is to truth. But with her, there is no gambling. Her royal station on "the marble floor" is above the workings of chance. She is true, and though her ways may be hard to understand at times, they are not a matter of chance.

In this first stanza we are given a brief but richly suggestive portrait of the Queen of Heaven who, when a voice calls her from the "gambling room," simply smiles and walks the other way. The last two lines merely intimate the approaching inevitable destruction of Black Diamond Bay.

The next five stanzas then proceed with the story, the tragedy, of the modern soul who has missed the last ship by choosing to remain where it is.

> As the mornin' light breaks open, the Greek comes down
> And he asks for a rope and a pen that will write
> "Pardon, monsieur," the desk clerk says
> Carefully removes his fez
> "Am I hearin' you right?"

The Greek spirit in man was Aristotelian logic in its glorious youth, but it has since grown up to become Copernican astronomy and now, having matured into senility, it has become logical positivism, or modern empirical science. This same spirit that can make the big bombs and lusts after such things as bio-engineering is the same spirit that necessarily leads to suicide. Having lost the knowledge of man as a spiritual being, life under this spirit has ultimately no meaning. This spirit, tragically lacking in spiritual consciousness, is the 'spirit' of our day and a dominant cultural force, and is here personified as "the Greek."

The desk clerk, on the other hand, represents the worldly scholar, or the academic aspect of research that plays such a dominant role of our modern consciousness. Aware that the Greek is tending toward suicide, about all the desk clerk can do is take off his hat and wonder, "do I understand you right, you want to commit suicide?" Then, this stanza goes on to give us the tragic relationship of this decrepit Greek spirit to Wisdom.

> And as the yellow fog is liftin'
> The Greek is quickly headin' for the second floor
> She passes him on the spiral staircase
> Thinkin' he's the Soviet Ambassador
> She starts to speak, but he walks away
> As the storm clouds rise and the palm branches sway
> On Black Diamond Bay

But now, just when the "yellow fog" of existential dread and despair of our recent history is beginning to lift, the Greek nevertheless continues to rush headlong toward his inevitable doom. It is too late for him, and as he passes "Her" on the "spiral staircase," he no longer recognizes her. In a sense, the final degradation of this Greek spirit is the "dialectical materialism" that became the soul of the Soviet system in the political life of the world. Small wonder then that she is thinking he is the Soviet Ambassador.

In the next stanza, three separate scenes occurring at different locations in the hotel are pictured as happening simultaneously, at that moment when lightning strikes, which causes the lights to go out. Our attention is directed from the lobby to the second floor, and finally to the gambling room.

> A soldier sits beneath the fan
> Doin' business with a tiny man who sells him a ring
> Lightning strikes, the light blows out

> The desk clerk wakes and begins to shout
> "Can you see anything?"
> Then the Greek appears on the second floor
> In his bare feet with a rope around his neck
> While the loser in the gambling room lights up a candle
> Says, "Open up another deck"
> But the dealer says, "Attendez-vous, s'il vous plait"
> As the rain beats down and the cranes fly away
> From Black Diamond Bay.

The living Spirit can use nature to accomplish its ends. First the moon faded away, then storm clouds arose, and now lightning strikes and rain beats down. In this stanza, the disaster clearly commences. The soldier and the tiny man picture forth the military-industrial complex, or the power-structure of this late stage of civilization. When the lights go out, the desk clerk finally becomes alarmed. In the gambling room, the loser doesn't want to give up the game, while the Greek on the second floor prepares for suicide. The dealer says to the gambler, "Please, wait."

As the tension mounts in the next stanza, panic breaks out. We see the relationship of militarism to Wisdom, and the woman is further characterized.

> The desk clerk heard the woman laugh
> As he looked around the aftermath and the soldier got tough
> He tried to grab the woman's hand
> Said, "Here's a ring, it cost a grand"
> She said, "That ain't enough"
> Then she ran upstairs to pack her bags

> While a horse-drawn taxi waited at the curb
> She passed the door that the Greek had locked
> Where a hand-written sign read, "Do Not Disturb"
> She knocked upon it anyway
> As the sun went down and the music did play
> On Black Diamond Bay

The woman laughs because a natural disaster is no threat to her. She can't be destroyed, only ignored. The soldier, the military aspect of the ego, makes a grab for her, offering her the ring he's gotten in his deal with the tiny man. It cost a grand, but that's not enough. She runs upstairs to get ready to leave. There is always a "horse-drawn" carriage at her disposal. The image of the horse again relates to intelligence as a carrying force. She makes one more attempt to get through to the Greek who does not want to be disturbed. The modern consciousness does not like to be disturbed by the mysterious reality of spirit because it cannot control it. So, the sun goes down and the music, the cosmic music, plays a tune of destruction on Black Diamond Bay.

In the next stanza, while she is trying one last time to reach the Greek, he chooses suicide over opening the door, and at that moment the volcano erupts.

> "I've got to talk to someone quick!"
> But the Greek said, "Go away," and he kicked the chair to the floor
> He hung there from the chandelier
> She cried, "Help, there's danger near
> Please open the door!"
> Then the volcano erupted
> And the lava flowed down from the mountain high above

> The soldier and the tiny man were crouched in
> the corner
> Thinking of forbidden love
> But the desk clerk said, "It happens every day"
> As the stars fell down and the fields burned
> away
> On Black Diamond Bay.

The Greek hangs himself from the chandelier, from the ornate, expensive, surrogate lights of conventional, quasi-scientific knowledge. There is danger near, the danger of destruction, but Sophia needs the human ego to open the door to Her if that destruction is to be avoided. The Greek spirit as the dominant force in modern consciousness, now grown senile, refuses to answer her call. He kicks the chair out from under and the volcano erupts, sending the purifying lava down from the mountain above. At this climactic moment, the soldier and the tiny man are caught in their compromised position of selfish love, moon-ego love, love of power and wealth. When the desk clerk says that it happens every day, there are two meanings suggested. One is that the worldly scholar would like to think that nothing out of the ordinary is really happening, that this is only another disturbance of the moment like so many others in history. The other is that on the level of individual consciousness, suicide out of desperation does indeed happen everyday.

Stanza six is the denouement of "the hard-luck story," but not the end of the tale this song tells. In the midst of the destruction of Black Diamond Bay something ineffable and mystical also occurs:

> As the island slowly sank
> The loser finally broke the bank in the gambling
> room

> The dealer said, "It's too late now
> You can take your money, but I don't know how
> You'll spend it in the tomb"
> The tiny man bit the soldier's ear
> As the floor caved in and the boiler in the basement blew
> While she's out on the balcony, where a stranger tells her
> "My darling, je vous aime beaucoup"
> She sheds a tear and then begins to pray
> As the fire burns on and the smoke drifts away
> From Black Diamond Bay

The end is near, the island is sinking, and the loser finally gets lucky. But it's too late now. At the same instant, the soldier and the tiny man have a disgusting last minute grapple for power. The floor caves in and the boiler blows. But on the balcony, which is to say, in "Her" realm high above the physical destruction, a stranger says to her, "I love you very much." Whereas the onset of this destruction only produced a carefree laugh, the love she finally receives from this "stranger" brings a tear of deep reverent joy.

In six stanzas, Dylan has told us – not with words only, but with pictures made of words – the story of the tragic fate of modern desacralized consciousness. If man does not wake up to the spiritual reality of life, he will reap destruction. This is similar to one of the major themes in William Irwin Thompson's book, *Time Falling Bodies Take To Light*:

> The shadow which our technological civilization casts is that of Lilith, "the Maid of Desolation" who dances in the ruins of cities....

> When man will not deal with Isis, through the path of initiation, he must deal with Lilith....
>
> Lilith has returned. To effect a reconciliation with her, man must not seek to rape the feminine and keep it under him. If he seeks to continue his domination of nature through genetic engineering and the repression of the spiritual, he will ensure that the only release from his delusions can come from destruction. Lilith will then dance in the ruins of Western civilization. But if man can accept initiation to see that Lilith is his long-lost primordial wife, then the energies of destruction can be transmuted and taken up into the creative destructuring of the old civilization, the industrial civilization that humanity has already outgrown.

But this story of inevitable destruction, which Dylan gives us in the first **six** stanzas is not the ultimate end of the story. The scenario the poet gives us in these six stanzas unfolds like a third-person novel, and then stanza seven begins suddenly with the first-person pronoun "I." This is the I of the poet, of course, but it is also the I-quality of the individual consciousness, the "witness," the very God-part of our being, the center of awareness, which through the path of initiation raises itself above the devastation. There is an uncanny ironic tone to this last stanza. The prosaic, almost blasé details of this stanza contrast as much with the tragic details of the first six stanzas as the first-person does with the third-person. Perhaps this all contributes to producing the effect of waking up from a dream.

> I was sittin' home alone one night in L.A.
> Watchin' old Cronkite on the seven o'clock news,
> It seems there was an earthquake that
> Left nothin' but a Panama hat
> And a pair of old Greek shoes
> Didn't seem like much was happenin'
> So I turned it off and went to grab another beer
> Seems like every time you turn around
> There's another hard-luck story that you're gonna hear
> And there's really nothin' anyone can say
> And I never did plan to go anyway
> To Black Diamond Bay

If you have understood the lyrics of the first six stanzas, then you will appreciate a wry humor in this last one. Going to get another beer is not an indication of heartless disregard for human suffering. If that were the case, Dylan never would have troubled himself to write and record this song. It is an amusingly ironic indication of how the I of this song, who "never did plan to go anyway," can go on with his life far removed from the destruction. After all, the moon-ego has already died and this "I" is conscious of its spiritual reality, or of what Emerson called "the infinitude of the private man." This hard-luck story of an earthquake and/or volcano that leaves nothing but a Panama hat and a pair of old Greek shoes is not news to this transcendental I. It's the same old story that has been told over and over again in history, from ancient times right up to the present.

"Black Diamond Bay" is a lyrical poem, a ballad, and also much more. It is a masterpiece work of art, which even if it does not fit nicely into some snug literary genre, nevertheless tells in a new and effective way the epic tale of our time. It would be a shame not to recognize the grandeur of this literary work of art just because the poet recorded it as a rock and roll song.

One of the great ironies of Dylan's career is that he has been so well rewarded in terms of fame and money and yet so little recognized for the great poet that he is. Thomas Merton, writing in 1967, said that, "Dylan may certainly have more in common with *Mad* comics than with Shakespeare but he is nevertheless definitely conscious of a poetic vocation and has communicated an authentic fervor to an audience that is deeply involved." But Merton, unfortunately, failed to appreciate the real nature of that vocation. During his early years, Dylan had met Carl Sandburg, Henry Miller, and Robert Graves, all men that Dylan respected. But those meetings were largely disappointments to Dylan because these brilliant older men could not *see* Dylan, for they were not aware that the "changing of the guards" had actually begun. Although those older writers had intimations that we are involved in a change larger than history, they were not prepared to see how Dylan figures in it.

The poet in Dylan was at least recognized by the poet Robert Bly, who included two of Dylan's lyrics in the poetry anthology that he edited, along with James Hillman and Michael Meade, called *The Rag and Bone Shop of the Heart*. The poet Charles Wright, also gave a tip of the hat to Dylan when he titled one of his poems, "When You're Lost In Juarez, In The Rain, And It's Eastertime too," which is nearly a direct quote of the first two lines in Dylan's "Just Like Tom Thumb's Blues." Aside from such minor acknowledgements, Dylan has generally gone unrecognized by poets and non-poets alike. Nevertheless, he continued his work courageously, guided by the inner light of his own intuition. One has the sense that surrounded by coincidental fame and fortune and by all the distractions of life in the midst of the media, Dylan pursued his craft, his special task, with the dedication of a lonely medieval monk. In 1985,

Dylan recorded a song called "Dark Eyes" in which a sense of this lonely dedication comes across. These lines deserve to be read closely:

> Oh, the gentlemen are talking and the midnight moon is on the riverside
> They're drinking up and walking and it's time for me to slide
> I live in another world where life and death are memorized
> Where the earth is strung with lovers' pearls and all I see are dark eyes
>
> A cock is crowing far away and another soldier's deep in prayer
> Some mother's child has gone astray, she can't find him anywhere
> But I can hear another drum beating for the dead that rise
> Whom nature's beast fears as they come and all I see are dark eyes.
>
> They tell me to be discreet for all intended purposes
> They tell me revenge is sweet and from where they stand, I'm sure it is
> But I feel nothing for their game where beauty goes unrecognized
> All I feel is heat and flame and all I see are dark eyes.
>
> Oh, the French girl, she's in paradise and a drunken man is at the wheel

> Hunger pays a heavy price to the falling gods of speed and steel
> Oh, time is short and the days are sweet and passion rules the arrow that flies
> A million faces at my feet but all I see are dark eyes

In these lyrics there is a sense of distance, an almost aching sense of the spiritual distance that separates the poet from most of his contemporaries. Because of this distance, the poet has continually come up against general miscomprehension, symbolized by the "dark eyes" that seem to meet him almost everywhere. His dedication has been to his work, to his creative activity, and he had understood from the beginning the limitations of his art. As he sang in "To Ramona" in 1964:

> And there's no use in tryin'
> T' deal with the dyin'
> Though I cannot explain that in lines

He not busy being born is busy dying, but it's for himself and his friends that Dylan's "stories" are sung. There is no use in trying to deal with the dying, or trying to explain about the "holy slow train." How can the dying make sense of such lines as this from "Idiot Wind"?

> There's a lone soldier on the cross, smoke pourin' out of a boxcar door
> You didn't know it, you didn't think it could be done, in the final end he won the wars
> After losin' every battle

We are at a parting of the ways where our old men dream dreams and our young men see visions. Young and old are here not a matter of years but a matter of the difference between *dreams* and *visions*. Dreams are rooted in the past and are egocentric; a vision, on the other hand, is a figurative foreshadowing of the future that visits Daimonic consciousness.

"Old men" are those who are unaware that the "guards" have changed and that the self-centeredness upon which dreams are based has been exploded. The "young men" are those who are capable of joining in as "friends" to celebrate the visions of this *minstrel of the dawn*. There are other "minstrels of the dawn" of course, but Dylan seems to be the one who has seen the visions most clearly and expressed them with uncommon power. If art is, as William Irwin Thompson said, a tone of voice, then the chief criterion for distinguishing the differences among artistic voices is that pointed out by Ralph Waldo Emerson when he wrote, "The tone of seeking is one, and the tone of having is another." The tone of having in Dylan's art is the uncanny source of its power.

This blue-eyed son of Queen Mary told us in 1963 that he'd "been ten thousand miles in the mouth of a graveyard," and so he *knew* that it was a Hard Rain that was going to fall. Twenty-two years later in the midst of that Hard Rain he tells us quietly and frankly in "Dark Eyes" that he lives in another world where life and death are memorized, that he hears another drum. And this other drum beats for the dead that rise, the ones who are courageous enough to enter the turbulent space, the ones who break the bondage of nature to behold The Mother. And these brave ones are therefore the ones that "nature's beast fears." These are the "young" ones who see visions, who see the lone soldier on a cross and the boxcar coming up around the bend. They see the One who wins the wars after having lost every battle, the One who said, "The truth shall set you free."

And freedom is the goal. But freedom is in the spirit. The kingdom of heaven is within, and only there in paradise will you find that "the French girl," that is, not the Statue of Liberty, but freedom itself. And when we are born in freedom, not only is The Mother "illuminated to us," but the Beautiful as well.

12

MAKE ROOM, THEN, FOR THE LIFE-GIVING ONES

> Every day the difference between the few and the many becomes sharper. A great yawning fissure divides the old from the new. There is still time perhaps to make the jump, but each day the hurdle becomes more perilous.
>
> – Henry Miller

"But what a poem means," wrote T.S. Eliot, "is as much what it means to others as what it means to the author; and indeed, in the course of time a poet may become merely a reader in respect to his own works, forgetting his original meaning – or without forgetting, merely changing." A poem is born from the soul of a poet where the unique individual comes together with the mysterious Universal in an act of sacred love. The authorship of the poem is never merely the limited individual, and the poem itself, once completed and released by the poet, has a life and destiny of its own. It enters into manifold relationships with human beings across time and space.

Many today are still reluctant to recognize Bob Dylan as a poet or to view his work as poetry in the best and highest sense of the word. Dylan was also reluctant to use the word "poet" in regard to himself, but for rather different reasons. As he said in 1966, "I don't call myself a poet because I don't like the word. I'm a trapeze artist." His electrifying blend of words, music and performance is, like all great art, a delicate feat performed in the air above the earth. If not poems in a strictly pedantic sense, his songs are nevertheless, like all great poetry, an artistic effort that aims at "the expression of the greatest emotional intensity of its time, with Beauty and Truth as guardian angels," to use T. S. Eliot's words.

Dylan didn't like the word "poet," one imagines, because poetry like all other aspects of modern spiritual life shows definite signs of decadence in the "Hard Rain" confusions of modern times. For the great poets and artists of the early part of the 20th century, art was their religion. But so much has happened since then through the proliferation of technology to trivialize anything remotely connected with the sacred, that art and the artist have become different things than they once were. Henry Miller, in his prophetic essay, "Of Art and the Future," spoke about the new role of art:

> To put it simply, art is only a stepping-stone to reality; it is the vestibule in which we undergo the rites of initiation. Man's task is to make of himself a work of art. The creations which man makes manifest have no validity in themselves; they serve to awaken, that is all. And that, of course, is a great deal. But it is not the all. Once awakened, everything will reveal itself to man as creation. Once the blinders have been removed and the fetters unshackled, man will

have no need to recreate through the elect cult of genius. Genius will be the norm.

Of course, we are not yet there in that future where genius is the norm. Rather, we are in a transitional period where the guards have only just begun to change. Miller belongs to the beginning of the 20th century as Dylan belongs to the end of it. Dylan is a sign of the coming change in art, which Henry Miller viewed prophetically:

> The floods of destruction sweep high and low; we are all part and parcel of the same mold; we have all been abetting the crime of man against man. The type of man we represent will be drowned out utterly. A new type will arise, out of the dregs of the old.... The era of neuters is drawing to a close. With the establishment of a new and vital polarity we shall witness *the birth of male-and-female in every individual*. What then portends in the realm of art is truly unthinkable. (Emphasis added.)

No, Dylan is not a poet in the traditional sense. Yet, by forging his works of art out of words and music and personal vocal articulations, he calls to mind the 12th century *Troubadours* of Provence, whose love songs are generally held to be the original wellspring of all modern lyric poetry. Robert Briffault wrote in his book *The Troubadours* that *Troubadour* songs were written in the vernacular, the common language of the day. Their "sighs and mannered tropes" and their "mincing measures of love" were characterized by the achievement of compression:

> For its effect it relied on the right word in the right place, not like Petrarch and the Elizabethans, on ornament.

This element of compression is one of the things that can make Dylan's work, like modern poetry, seem difficult. As Briffault so quaintly put it in his book:

> ...compression draws more largely on the attention of the reader, accustomed, in our over-excited age, to literary cake which levels down to his quick luncheon habits, and he feels injured when unable to snap up at one bite the meat of a period or a page.

The achievement of compression in many of Dylan's songs is an extraordinary thing. It has that wonderful quality that calls upon the audience to be co-creators. Of course, no one is under any obligation to involve himself so deeply in Dylan's art. However, doing so turns out to be its own reward. Approach it with a believing soul and you will certainly find something more than "literary cake."

Dylan, as a modern *Troubadour*, calls to mind as well the Sufi mystic poetry which inspired the 12th century *Troubadours* in that the heart of his work is the expression of a mystical quest. But Dylan is no more a Sufi than he is a poet. The hallmark of his career is the steadfast refusal to be hampered by any tradition, though strong echoes from many traditions appear in his work. In 1966, he said of his work, "The songs are insanely honest, not meaning to twist any heads, and written only for the reason that I myself me alone wanted and needed to write them."

This uncompromisingly personal strategy has been the source of much that is enigmatic in his songs, yet it has also been the source of their real power. His songs ring true because they reflect the honest and active inner life of an authentic person, one who is awake to the infinitude of the private man. The riddle-like nature of many of his lyrics has caused some to compare them to parables while prompting others to accuse Dylan of perpetrating a hoax. But Dylan comes to his audience first through his music and performance. These accurately reflect the visceral reactions to the experience of life in our materialistic culture shared by his audience. From these shared feelings, his audience can gradually move on toward an awareness of the Vision that informs his lyrics. As one begins to see into the riddles, one begins to have increasing respect for the amazingly consistent and unified perspective of that Vision.

Dylan has written many different kinds of songs, but they are all informed by the same Vision, a Vision which, as it deepened, became more definitively Christocentric. But Christ as the consummate individual, is the unity of the Logos or the Word, and Sophia or Wisdom, and Dylan's mystical quest of his Vision led ultimately to the mystery of the "I."

In the early years of his career, the actual depth of Dylan's Vision was not much appreciated. In the turbulent decade of the 1960s, he was often thought of as a topical protest songwriter. This inclination to see him as a social critic and/or political rebel was not without some foundation since there is a point of convergence where his lyrics and social protest meet. To the extent that the social protest movements of the 1960s sought to reinstate the concept of the dignity of man as a spiritual being, as a son of the Father, they resonated with Dylan's lyrics. Or, to put it another way, Dylan was often able to give powerful expression to the longings of the protest movements because his lyrics sprang from the insight into man's spiritual dimension upon which the moral justification of the protest movements ultimately rested. Social protest, though it is one element of Dylan's work, is more peripheral than central.

What is central to Dylan's work, even if it was not immediately apparent, is the Good News of man's divinity. Christ, the divine and eternal Son, is the Logos, the Word. That is, He is the living, cosmic sign or emblem of the Great All by which the otherwise unknown Father is revealed. It is by this Word that knowledge passes – knowledge which is first and last self-knowledge. Christ incarnated in the man Jesus to make it possible for all men to know the truth about themselves. Only in Him and through Him, like Jesus, can I realize that I am a son of the Father. But any attempt to express this Good News in ordinary words is bound to sound hollow and abstract. There is a great deal of difference between the dry formulaic words, which are used to express this good news, and the living experience of realizing its truth as a matter of *gnosis,* as self-knowledge. The living experience is born from the blood, sweat and tears of an existential moment, of a descent into the turbulent space of the mystery of one's own being. We are called into that mysterious and turbulent space by the hidden Wisdom, or Sophia, where sublime Truth, Beauty and Goodness underlie the reality of our own souls. On this inward journey, our love for Her is tested, and we are put to the proof. In this testing, we undergo a death of the ego and a rebirth in the Holy Spirit. Reborn in the Holy Spirit we enter the primordial mystery of the "I" where we discover the truth of Christ's words, "He that findeth his life shall lose it: and he that loseth his life for my sake shall find it." We lose the life of the moon-ego, the *Joker*, to find our greater and more abundant life in the spirit.

In childhood, faith is a fact, even if an unconscious one. As yet unacquainted with the world, the child's imagination is wholly integrated with life, and so play, creativity, is the order of the day. The break occurs gradually as the stormy sea of emotions awakens and as the necessity of work and the overwhelming confusions of the world press in upon him. Some degree of agnosticism or unbelief eventually invades the soul. Many never find a way back, but most come sooner or later to some sort of private renewal of faith and reconciliation with the mystery of life that is more or less a matter of conscious decision.

This pattern of unconscious faith, loss of faith, and then consciously renewed faith governs the progress of the human race as well as the individual. In a sense, the spiritual crisis of our time is not unlike the mid-life crisis of the individual wavering between suicide and rebirth. This "dark night of the soul" is the pre-condition for human freedom, for that spiritual maturity when childish things are at last put aside.

For man is a creature born out of desire into duty, out of the spirit into the world. Desire and duty are the poles of that chaos, which is the darkness of earthly life, of earth-bound consciousness. This chaos is the crucible in which the self is tried, the cross on which the earthly ego hangs. For man there is no escape until he acknowledges the Creator.

When he can say at last with his heart, "Father, into Thy hands I commend my spirit," he gives up the ghost of a separate earthly ego. For the new man that arises in the soul, the spiritual man, the discord of desire and duty becomes harmonized as love, and the spirit and the world become resolved into one.

For mankind as a whole, it is much the same. With art, mankind is bound by desire to the individual. With science, mankind is bound by duty to the world. But when the artist fails to acknowledge the Creator, art degenerates into an obsession with the earthly ego and leads ultimately to individual suicide. When science fails to acknowledge the Creator, it becomes an obsession with power and leads finally to collective suicide.

This is the crossroads we have reached in the Hard Rain confusion of modern times. We must now change or pay more for remaining the same. "We are right in the middle," wrote William Irwin Thompson, "of the climax of human evolution and yet most people cannot see it." To use Thompson's words, we are moving from a worn-out, post-industrial culture toward the planetization of culture for which a change of consciousness is needed, a change from economics to ecology as the governing science, and a change from ego-consciousness to Daimonic consciousness, Daimonic in the sense of the inner guide Socrates experienced and called his *Daimon*. The part of our consciousness that is multidimensional, or out of the ego's conventional construction of time and space, is the *Daimon*. The emergence of Daimonic consciousness in Dylan takes the feminine form of Sophia/Psyche, which guided him toward an experience of Christ-consciousness.

The progress of spiritual life, i.e. the evolution of consciousness, whether in the individual or for mankind generally, is characterized by the increasing awareness of being. When something that lives in the preconscious arises and takes form for the first time in consciousness, it is an illumination that deepens the awareness of being. As mankind's evolution proceeds, some individuals are destined, it seems, to push beyond that point attained by mankind generally. Dylan is such an individual, and in this way comes near to being something of a prophet, not so much by forecasting future events as by boldly "pioneering" beyond the bounds of common contemporary consciousness and reporting his "tales of yankee power" with inspirational force.

What Dylan has experienced is a matter of *gnosis*, of self-knowledge, and he knows that, by and by, more and more people will experience a similar awakening in some form or other. This slow, gradual process of spiritual transformation is "the holy slow train" coming up around the bend through the "Hard Rain" of contemporary spiritual confusion. The mystical dimensions to which Dylan's lyrics testify live in all of us in varying degrees of consciousness. In his art, woven of words, music and performance, they are expressed with such originality and power and courage that they resonate subliminally in the souls of his audience. And so it happens that Dylan, despite the spiritual havoc of our times, becomes a cult figure. Our barely conscious but crucial spiritual hunger finds its living reflection in what has come into the world through him.

Today when so many poets are ensnared in specious discussions about the "failure of nerve," "the breakdown of communication," and so forth, Dylan wittingly or not, went back to the *Troubadour* beginnings of lyric poetry to start fresh, producing a body of work that has not only brought him fame and fortune, but which penetrates the layers of confusion and the junkyard wreckage of tradition to touch the hearts of millions. True, many of his fans have only the merest inkling about what the words mean or where he is really coming from, but they *experience* his songs and by "deep calling to deep" a connection is made. The images and the Vision from which they are born ride on the music and the voice into the unconscious, and then mysteriously they draw many to listen again and again. And as happens with great poetry, with repeated exposure, something new and deeper is always discerned. Dylan, by melding his poems to ostensibly popular music, overcomes the isolation of the modern poet imprisoned in tradition.

The Orphic impulse of "don't look back" has been a constant feature of Dylan's career. He has been "pressin' on" continually without much regard for how well he was being understood, confident that if his work is true, it will eventually find its mark. As he sang in "Restless Farewell,"

> But if the arrow is straight
> And the point is slick
> It can pierce through dust no matter how thick

Dylan's whole career shines forth as an extraordinary example of the power of faith, faith in his own spiritual essence and in the spiritual as the ground of reality. Like Odysseus passing through the Strait of Messina, he has *survived*. He has survived, on the one hand, Charybdis: that whirlpool that would suck our souls into oblivion and non-existence; and on the other, Scylla: that monster who would take us into her dark cave to suffer the hellish dismemberment of insanity. Dylan has survived; he has maintained the integrity of self against the crushing whirlpool of the god-forsaken world *and* from the many forms of personal insanity that can result from a total withdrawal from the world. Neither losing himself in the world nor permitting the world to lose him by a retreat into apathy, he has achieved that delicate balance of being in the world, yet not of it.

It is that delicate balance that produces the well-known elusiveness surrounding Dylan. Call him what you will, he is apt to say that he is just another songwriter, a singer or guitar player, or that he is no different from anyone else. And on one level, that is exactly correct, but not the whole story. The elusive quality of Dylan's presence in the world reminds me a little bit of that story about Jesus who, when he was about to be stoned, "went out of the temple, going through the midst of them, and so passed by."

In any event, if Dylan is not a poet, he is a poetic spirit and a creative artist whose work reveals a man of profound faith. As Henry Miller once wrote:

> Back of every creation, supporting it like an arch, is faith ... Men who know and believe

> can foresee the future. They don't want to put something over – they want to put something *under* us ... We are not kept alive by legislators and militarists, that's fairly obvious. We are kept alive by men of faith, men of vision ... Make room, then, for the life-giving ones!

For me, Dylan is a man of faith, a man of vision, one of the life-giving ones. His lyrics have been an important force in my life, not simply because they are inspirational but also because in many a dark moment they helped me to see the light. I am grateful to Dylan for his work, which for me is a living poetry and a "poetry of the stars." If I consider Dylan one of the great men of our time, it is not to make of him a hero to worship, for one must remember what Emerson wrote in "Uses of Great Men":

> All that respects the individual is temporary and prospective, like the individual himself, who is ascending out of his limits into a catholic existence. We have never come at the true and best benefit of any genius, so long as we believe him an original force. In the moment when he ceases to help us as a cause, he begins to help us more as an effect. Then he appears as an exponent of a vaster mind and will. The opaque self becomes transparent with the light of the First Cause.

CODA: LIFTING THE VEIL
(IF ONLY A LITTLE)

> I don't think I'm gonna be really understood until maybe one hundred years from now. What I've done, what I am doing, nobody else does or has done. When I'm dead and gone maybe people will realize that, and then figure it out. I don't think anything I've done has been even mildly hinted at.
>
> -Bob Dylan

As Virtual Reality more and more tints and distorts our environment, it becomes the new contour of that great divide separating the old from the new, and the many from the few, over which there may yet be just time enough for one to make the jump.

The thing about virtual reality is how it subtracts geography from the equation, severing us from our roots in the earth. Where we come from no longer seems to be of any significance whatsoever. Time, as we know it, is a function of the earth, of the rotation of the earth and its relationship to the other heavenly bodies. When we are cut off from our roots in the earth, time itself changes.

Time hasn't actually stopped, though it certainly *feels* like it has. Because our ties to the earth have been uprooted, time no longer flows, it freezes. The earth is a body in outer space, not in cyberspace. Cyberspace isn't space at all. Like the spirit, it is a spaceless place, only it is a *dead* spaceless place, a lifeless spaceless-ness, a spiritual vacuum. As such, the arising of cyberspace signifies a counterfeit stoppage of time.

Cyberspace is where a soul would go to die, if it could die.

In our new virtual reality, life has gone into hyper-cybernation; we have largely surrendered ourselves to the machine and to the rule of mechanical processes. The "Bear Mountain Picnic" has at last become that kind of "Massacre" it was all along designed to be, where "There's a bran' new gimmick every day/Just to take somebody's money away." You have only to look again at Bob Dylan's "Talking Bear Mountain Picnic Massacre Blues" from 1962 to feel how we are now frozen in time. More accurately, we have become frozen in a specific period of time, in that infamous 20th Century, the notorious American Century – no matter what the calendar says.

For it is we who have stopped – not time.

When we come to a stop, time itself freezes, and that particular time period we then find ourselves in instantly crystallizes into a new kind of "city" in cyberspace. "The 20th Century" is the name of that cyber city where we now find ourselves abiding, dawdling about on the very edge of history. When time freezes, clocks and calendars can only lie. It may be 2011, but it's still the 20th Century. And a 20th Century by any other name would still be a 20th Century. This cyber city is now *The City* of man, where we all happen to live.

It is much like a great medieval walled fortress, this city, with guards posted at all the gates. Only here the guards are standing their posts on the inside of the gates, not on the outside, for the Lords of the Castle are concerned that the electronic peasantry should not escape. There is not much chance of that, anyway. Already a person could travel the information superhighway his whole life and never even see a gate.

Coda: Lifting The Veil (If Only A Little)

For anyone who still has a hankering for "the wild, unknown country," there is only one way out. That way is up, and the only way up is to learn what stopping time really means.

When you really stop time, you still go on living, only in a new and unforeseen dimension. When you are the one who has stopped time, the magic and mystery of life become more palpable than ever before, not less. When you stop time, you discover eternity to be your real home where your heart's always in the Highlands high above The City. You no longer feel claustrophobically condemned to wander aimlessly around in this world as if it were "another goddamned shopping mall," to borrow a phrase from an old Dan Folgelberg song.

On the other hand, when it is you who have come to a stop, when it is you who have come to a standstill, time merely freezes into place.

But if you don't stop, if you manage to go on moving toward that grand accomplishment of stopping time, then you will eventually awaken into a new life where the conversation is all, to use Martin Buber's phrase, "A Dialogue Above the City." If you manage to rediscover your roots in the earth, and thereby rediscover real time, then there is every possibility that you will also learn what it means to stop time. Then you will know that life is more than this passage from birth to death. For once you have found out what stopping time really means, you will always be busy being born.

* * *

There is no doubt that I could easily make this book two or three times longer by continuing to explicate the extraordinary number of lyrics that Dylan has continued to write and record while we were being taxied into the new millennium. His three major albums that span the nominal end of the 20th century and the beginning of the 21st, *Oh, Mercy, Time Out of Mind,* and *"Love and Theft,"* would certainly lend themselves nicely to this procedure. Even the title of this last album suggests that it was right to begin this study of Dylan's lyrics with "The Thief Who Kindly Spoke." The "thief," as the conscience, has always been central to the spiritual love this mystical poet has been singing about from the beginning.

In any case, the chief premises of this book would only be further confirmed by continuing with the exercise of explication. That Dylan's lyrics constitute a solid and unified body of poetic expression, and that the mystery language he has created reveals a mystical poet uniquely important to this period of cultural transition, would remain unchanged. Besides, any reader who feels an affinity for approaching Dylan's lyrics in this vein will enjoy experiencing Dylan's more recent creations "again for the first time" on their own.

Instead, my purpose in this "Coda" will be to round out my study of Dylan's lyrics by lifting the veil, if only a little, on the deepest mystery concerning Dylan's particular kind of art: *his artistic conscience.* We will do that by zooming in on some of the intimate specifics pertaining to the psycho-spiritual alchemy at work in his creative labors.

There is no doubt that Dylan views himself as an artist. It could also be said that this view was loudly reaffirmed, even if only superficially, when Time magazine included Dylan in its selection of the 100 most influential people of the 20th century. He was included under the category of "Artists and Entertainers."

But that's just the rub. Is Dylan truly an artist, or only an extremely clever entertainer? What is art, anyway? What is it that artists do, and why do we honor it? What kind of artist is Bob Dylan?

Coda: Lifting The Veil (If Only A Little)

There are those who might quibble over whether or not Bob Dylan is really an artist, but few would have any problem with calling him a "genius." However, here in The City of the 20th Century, in this time-frozen space of our cyber city, who even knows any more what "genius" really means?

Bob Dylan has probably never referred to himself as a "genius." He has, though, fairly consistently referred to himself as an artist – even if only with that not quite tongue-in-cheek phrase: "trapeze-artist." What did he mean by that, what kind of artist does he really think he is?

In 1977 Bob Dylan was interviewed by Allen Ginsberg, who intended to write a critical appraisal of the film, *Renaldo And Clara*, that Dylan was then editing. Ginsberg never wrote the piece, but a record of the discussion was printed in an anthology called *The Dylan Companion*, published in 1990. In that exchange, Dylan tried to explain to Ginsberg what it is that artists are striving to do. He told Ginsberg, "We try to make something better out of what is real. If we want to be successful as an artist, we make it better, and give meaning to something meaningless." Ginsberg then asked Dylan, "What's your idea of 'better' – your direction of 'better'?" Dylan answered:

> You can make something lasting. You wanna stop time, that's what you wanna do. You want to live forever, right, Allen? Huh? In order to live forever you have to stop time. In order to stop time you have to exist in the moment, so strong as to stop time and prove your point. So that you have stopped time. And if you succeed in doing that, everyone who comes into contact with what you've done – whatever it might be, whether you've carved a statue or painted a painting – will catch some of that;

> they'll recognize that you have stopped time —
> they won't realize it, but that's what they will
> recognize, that you have stopped time. That's
> a heroic feat.

Clearly, then, Dylan's own conception of art has to do with stopping time, and the accomplishment of this feat is viewed as "heroic." He also seems to say that if the artist succeeds in existing so strongly in the moment that he stops time, then whatever he has created will necessarily come into the world trailing clouds of glory, so to speak. It will come into the world bearing traces of the eternal along with it. It may well be that those who come into contact with his creation will not themselves realize the eternal, or the stopping of time. However, they will sense that the power in this work of art has come from the artist who has accomplished that heroic feat of stopping time.

In this same interview, Ginsberg also asked Dylan, "Do you want to be immortal? And why?" Who knows what Ginsberg expected Dylan to reply? This question would be simply silly and vain, unless, of course, Ginsberg was referring to Dylan's work. Dylan, like any artist, would naturally want his work to survive. Dylan's answer, however, is specially interesting because of the reference he made to something Henry Miller once wrote. Dylan said to Ginsberg:

> I'd like my work to survive, yeah. Do you
> remember what Henry Miller wrote on that!
> "An artist inoculates the world with his dis-
> illusionment." It's not good enough to be an
> observer all the time. You have to know that
> you've stopped time. You think about nothing.
> You're totally absorbed in what you're doing.

> Any singer can do that. Some fake it. When it resolves itself, it's never resolved – you have to resolve it. To resolve is nothing more than letting go.

As we go along we will be exploring these cryptic remarks that Dylan made in answer to Ginsberg's questions. We will consider them at some length in order to get a more precise picture of the specific nature of Dylan's art. Most importantly, we will pay close attention to the notion that the artist "inoculates the world with his disillusionment."

Before we proceed with that, however, it may be well to note something else that Henry Miller once wrote. It was in *The World Of Sex,* where he was attempting to reveal some of the messier and more mysterious personal details of his own experience of transformation.

"It was an ordeal which threatened never to end," he wrote. "Time dragged on in a way I had never thought possible. There were five-minute intervals which stretched out so painfully that I thought I would go mad."

At this point in his life's journey, Miller felt painfully trapped in his life-situation. We could say that he had not yet discovered how to stop time. Rather, we should say that he was feeling himself sinking into the quicksand of frozen time at that place where one knows, "You must either change, or pay more for remaining the same." He expressed this feeling of being up against a wall, of being backed into a corner: "My only recourse – I no longer had a choice – was to lose my identity."

"I gave out," he went on, "that I had left for Alaska, but the truth was that I remained only a few blocks away." In other words, he went into hiding. "I remained below a long time, oblivious of such things as food, fresh air, sunlight, human companionship." At last, though, he did manage to emerge.

Coming back to the surface, he expressed what had happened to him with the intriguing phrase, "In the depths I made contact with the earth spirits."

Among those he named as "earth spirits" was Ralph Waldo Emerson. It seems significant that Miller identified Emerson, along with some others, as an "earth spirit." "I understood their language," he explained. "I was at home with them." After thus discovering his roots in the earth, Miller was then able to begin moving out of, and beyond, that cul-de-sac of frozen time.

With his geography reestablished, Miller could begin to "get real," as we might say today. After making this contact with the earth spirits, Miller went on to say, "No valid reason why I should ever come up for air. I had the whole thing in my hands. But, like a lone prospector who stumbles upon a forgotten gold mine, I had to take what I could in my bare hands and come to the surface for assistance. It was imperative to convince others that such a treasure existed, beg them to return with me and help themselves to their heart's content."

And there we have it: Bob Dylan connects himself to Henry Miller, who has connected himself to Ralph Waldo Emerson. This is how we rediscover our roots in the earth. Emerson, to this day, is referred to as "The Sage Of Concord." In his own day, he was known as "The Wisest American." In cyberspace, it doesn't matter where you come from, but in real space, where time doesn't really stop until *you* have stopped it, you need to discover the roots that connect you to earth and to the life of the earth.

If Dylan never had much to say about genius, both Miller and Emerson did. Both were profoundly concerned with art, especially literary art, and with the idea of genius. Since these are Dylan's actual roots, let us consider what that connection may portend.

Coda: Lifting The Veil (If Only A Little)

Emerson had many astute and perceptive things to say about "genius." For instance, there is a book that was published after his death, which was a combination of notes and lectures he had given at Harvard, Cambridge and London, called *Natural History of the Intellect*. In this book you will find it written, "There are two theories of life; one for the demonstration of our talent, the other for the education of man."

No doubt people in The City, which is to say, those who are still stranded on the ice floes of the virtual 20th Century, are not apt to draw such fine distinctions. Nor is it to be expected that they have ever thought about the possibility that there may be such things as "theories of life," much less that there happens to be two of them.

Well, what is this life for, anyway? Are we given this life merely as an arena for displaying our innate talents while we are here, or is there something more to it? And what does Emerson mean by "the education of man?" He went on to elaborate about the two theories of life: that the purpose of life is for the demonstration of our talents or for the education of man.

> One is activity, the busybody, the following of that practical talent which we have, in the belief that what is so natural, easy and pleasant to us and desirable to others will surely lead us out safely; in this direction lie usefulness, comfort, society, low power of all sorts. The other is trust, religion, consent to be nothing for eternity, entranced waiting, the worship of ideas. This is solitary, grand, secular. They are in perpetual balance and strife. One is talent, the other genius. One is skill, the other character.

In other words, if you come down on the side of the theory that the purpose of life is primarily for the demonstration of our talents, then you will be moving along the road that leads toward "low power of all sorts." You will be more enamored of skill than of character. However, if you side with the theory that life is for the education of man, then your allegiance will go to "genius." By a willingness to be nothing for eternity, you consent to wait, entranced in "the worship of ideas," trusting the genius at work in your being. What is this dichotomy really about?

Emerson went on to say, "We are continually tempted to sacrifice genius to talent, the hope and promise of insight to the lust of a freer demonstration of those gifts which we have; and we buy this freedom to glitter by the loss of general health." In the cyber city of the 20th Century, this "freedom to glitter" seems to be all that life is about.

Naturally, there is always an "entertainment" element involved in art. And talent, of course, is a requirement. But when talent, always more plentiful than genius, becomes the major credit card for purchasing our attention, more often than not we will end up getting only what we have paid for, and almost never anything more. Talent by itself, like a Mastercard, may be good for a lot things, but it is useless when it comes to that which is priceless.

And what is priceless in art is the new life it brings into the world, a new life that does not arise out of the things of the world, or out of anything inherent in them. This new life is what can only spring forth from the deep mysterious life inherent in the character of the genius. Such new life is never merely entertaining, it is also revitalizing, restorative, and healthful. That is what Emerson means when he says that the price for "this freedom to glitter," this "lust," is the loss of general health.

Coda: Lifting The Veil (If Only A Little)

Genius is much more than a particular combination and concentration of effective talents. It's the channel for the actual delivery of insights through inspiration. It's what renews the life of the soul.

If the 20th Century, as many commentators are now wont to say, is the "American century," then Emerson's next paragraph, which was written even before that infamous century began, is telling:

> It is the levity of this country to forgive everything to talent. If a man show cleverness, rhetorical skill, bold front in the forum or senate, people clap their hands without asking more. We have a juvenile love of smartness, of showy speech. We like faculty that can rapidly be coined into money, and society seems to be in conspiracy to utilize every gift prematurely, and pull down genius to lucrative talent.

Here I am reminded of something I saw many years ago while working for the Post Office. I was sorting letters (everything was done by hand back then), and I noticed that the tray of mail I was working was all from the same company. Today, this company would likely be called a high-tech firm. At any rate, this company had its own meter machine that printed the company's name and slogan along with the postage. The slogan read: "If it doesn't sell, it's not creative." This narrow view of creativity blatantly boasts that the measure of creativity is its marketability. What could more succinctly summarize that pandemic "pulling down of genius to lucrative talent," which in this American century has been ratcheted up to a fevered pitch near insanity?

Well, after all, this is only what we have come to know and accept as the ways of the world, isn't it? To some extent, the triumph of talent over genius has always been with us, though never more so than in the American century.

It might well be said that Dylan was especially sensitive to this commercialization of talent at the expense of genius. It could also be said that he was cognizant early in his career that soon we would all experience the inevitable unleashing of an enormous and overwhelming array of profitable intellectual properties in every arena of society. And further, that he anticipated the disorientation we would all experience once this dam broke, engulfing whatever remained of our once seemingly stable culture. I am convinced this conspiracy of society "to utilize every gift prematurely" is what Bob Dylan referred to as "The Flood."

You may remember the line, "Well, it's sugar for sugar/ And salt for salt,/If you go down in the flood,/It's gonna be your fault." For those of us who came of age in the 1960s, there was probably no better early warning system than Bob Dylan's lyrics for sounding the alarm.

Talent and genius, according to Emerson, "are in perpetual balance and strife." This suggests that these two aspects of creativity constantly contend with each other, not only in society, but within the individual as well. Let us consider that the mythological names for these two may well be Cain and Abel. Cain's offerings were the things he had forged with his own hands, which could be thought of as expressions of his talent. Abel's offerings, on the other hand, were the fruits of his having faithfully husbanded the life forms or forces entrusted to him, which could be considered the expressions of his God-given genius. According to this mythical tale, God found Abel's offerings preferable, and then Cain, in anger, slew Abel. It is not so much that once upon a time Cain killed Abel, but that

Coda: Lifting The Veil (If Only A Little)

the Cain in us is continually killing the Abel in us. And as a result, a whole lot of "Cain" has been raised.

We need both, of course. These brothers are really brother aspects of our creative natures. Think of Dylan. Here is a man who was blessed with an astonishing array of talents, yet those talents have been exercised in the service of his genius. Despite the fact that his worldly success appears to rest on his obvious talents, it ultimately derives from the genius at work in him. The peculiar circumstance that his genius remains largely misunderstood and under-appreciated, even now in 2011, accounts for the uncanny and unusual quality of his fame. It is the extraordinary quality of that genius, however, that this book seeks to shed light on.

To lift the veil, if only a little, we will need to return to what Dylan told Ginsberg, "Do you remember what Henry Miller wrote on that! 'An artist inoculates the world with his disillusionment.'" What Dylan is alluding to will be found in Henry Miller's *Sexus*, the first volume of his "autobiographical" trilogy, *The Rosy Crucifixion*:

> A child has no need to write, he is innocent.
> A man writes to throw off the poison which he
> has accumulated because of his false way of life.
> He is trying to recapture his innocence, yet all
> he succeeds in doing (by writing) is to inoculate
> the world with the virus of his disillusionment.

The writer, the artist, is first of all a person like anyone else. And like everyone else, he comes eventually to experience life as discord. He is aware that something has gone wrong somewhere. He aims to understand it, and perhaps fix it. Somewhere along the line, the innocence he once knew as a child has simply slipped away and vanished. He is driven to write in order to come to grips with the discord, in the hope of finding his way back to that lost innocence.

More often than not, though, the picture of the world he presents to us will amount to no more than an artistically rendered judgment reflecting his own angst, the accumulated poison of his "false way of life," which he would like to rid himself of. All he may be doing, after all, is infecting an already troubled and chaotic world with his own reactionary and rationalistic brand of disenchantment.

Any creative person will sooner or later find himself confronting this difficulty. A person may feel that he has seen through the illusions that give rise to and support the evils and troubles of the world, and that it is his job to expose these illusions in order to set things right. The difficulty is, how can he ever be certain that the views he has arrived at are not merely different illusions, illusions rooted only in his private sense of discord? Henry Miller wrote about what his confrontation with this conundrum was like:

> The little phrase — *Why don't you try to write?* — involved me, as it had from the very beginning, in a hopeless bog of confusion. I wanted to enchant but not enslave; I wanted to free the imagination of all men at once because without the support of the whole world, without a world imaginatively unified, the freedom of the imagination becomes a vice. I had no respect for writing *per se* any more than I had for God *per se*. Nobody, no principle, no idea has validity in itself. What is valid is only that much of anything, God included — which is realized by all men in common.

Coda: Lifting The Veil (If Only A Little)

In Miller's view, the freedom of the imagination, which is the basis for all artistic endeavor, may easily turn into the vice of infecting the world with one's own personal sickness, unless it is anchored in a world imaginatively unified. The world can only be imaginatively unified by that which is realized by all men in common. Unified by anything less, the freedom of the imagination may only be a matter of self-deception resulting in the spread of a private virus-like disillusionment with life.

This is a problem for the inner conscience of the artist. He has to *feel* his way into those depths of being where the feelings are true and harmonize with "what is realized by all men in common." Otherwise, he can never have the confidence that his work rises above being, however inadvertently, merely the further infection of an already sick world. If he has sufficient talent, and the capacity of a free imagination, as well, it is true that he will be able to produce artistic work. But how will he ever know that this artistic work will also be a work of art? Any artist who is more interested in his art than in the mere display of his talents as a means for turning a profit, will eventually experience this dilemma.

Where can such a profoundly conscientious attitude toward art be found these days in the cyber city of the 20th Century? With the raging fires of the unanchored and free imagination being constantly stoked with the fuel of large potential earnings and quick payoffs from the numerous dynamos of mass markets and mass distribution systems, who any longer bothers about such philosophical niceties? "Time is of the essence; time is money; strike while the iron is hot," and so forth. "Make hay while the sun shines" – yada, yada, yada.

Only genius, willing to be nothing for eternity, would fuss over such scruples. Only genius, guided by the solitary worship of ideas, would be willing to wait entranced while the horde of hustlers and mountebanks storm society with their talent, cleverly cashing in on society's juvenile love of smartness. For only genius, abiding in trust, knows what life is really for: the education of man.

Miller wrestled and worked his way through this dilemma in order that his art might transcend the threat of being merely the inoculation of the world with the virus of his personal discontent. Dylan shared this deep artistic concern, this scruple of the genius, if you will, and so he was quick to allude to Miller's thought when he was discussing his ideas about art with Ginsberg. In his answers to Ginsberg, Dylan insisted that even if some were able to fake it, this dilemma was not truly resolvable without stopping time, and that this stopping of time somehow involved a "letting go."

Dylan's responses to Ginsberg were direct personal responses made by one poet to another. There is a certain elliptical quality at play in these exchanges that necessarily leaves room for interpretation. Whatever they may point to, however, they definitely concerned the stopping of time as the resolution of the dilemma inherent in artistic conscience. This solution has something to do with the artist resolving it by "letting go." To parcel out the meaning of this elliptical dialogue, let's return to the inoculation idea that Dylan referred to.

The artist takes to writing initially as a way of casting off the accumulated poison of his false way of life in the hope of recapturing the innocence of childhood. If he were still innocent, obviously there would be no need to write. By writing, though, he only infects the world with the virus of his own disillusionment, unless he manages to transcend the inherent pitfalls of the free imagination by anchoring his creative work in "what is realized by all men in common." This is the core struggle at work in the conscience of the artist.

Coda: Lifting The Veil (If Only A Little)

Why would anyone wish to put himself through such an arduous struggle, such a strange ordeal? Why not just live life as it comes? Miller also addressed this question in *Sexus*:

> If there is no realization, there is no purpose or advantage in substituting the imaginative life for the purely adventurous one of reality. Everyone who lifts himself above the activities of the daily round does so not only in the hope of enlarging his field of experience, or even of enriching it; but of quickening it. Only in this sense does the struggle have any meaning. Accept this view, and the distinction between failure and success is nil.

The artist is driven to recapture his innocence. He knows, perhaps at first only instinctively, that the way to this end begins with that quickening of life he experiences when he is engaged in the creative process. If realization were not a real possibility, if no breakthrough to reality were actually possible, then what sense would there be in foregoing the ordinary adventure of life for such an arduous, misty quest?

But if he is sincere and honest with himself, the quickening of life felt in the creative process will prove the strongest attraction. It will gradually draw him deeper and deeper into the mysteries of the creative process itself. For the artist, this "quickening of life" becomes the thing, while the outward success or failure of his artistic projects will always remain secondary. Miller goes on:

> And this is what every great artist comes to learn en route – that the process in which he is involved has to do with another dimension

> of life, that by identifying himself with this process he *augments* life. In this view of things he is permanently removed – and protected – from that insidious death which seems to triumph all about him.

The artist, in living his life for the process itself, experiences an augmentation of life into another dimension wherein he feels himself "permanently removed" from the round of ordinary death and dying, and even protected, in a certain sense, from its ordinary inevitability. The experience of this augmented life carries him into another dimension beyond death. In this other dimension of life he comes to an experience of the mystery that reveals something about the great secret. As Miller says:

> He divines that the great secret will never be apprehended but incorporated in his very substance. He has to make himself a part of the mystery, live in as well as with it.

The mysterious process of creativity is for the artist like the mystery of conception in the female human being. Once inspiration has taken hold, it forces upon the artist the same recognition that eventually assails every pregnant woman. Like the pregnant woman, the artist is compelled to recognize that life is bigger than who we are, and that if he already sincerely cares about the as-yet unborn life growing inside, there is nothing he can do but accept the mystery of it. He will have no choice but to accept that the mystery of what is going on within him may never become completely comprehensible. Nor can he try to hold back the process of creation until he has "comprehended" it. All he can do is learn to live with the mystery of it and let it come to fruition within him. Only to the extent

Coda: Lifting The Veil (If Only A Little)

he succeeds with living *in* as well as *with* it, will he make "the great discovery." As Miller says:

> Acceptance is the solution: it is an art, not an egotistical performance on the part of the intellect. Through art, one finally establishes contact with reality: that is the great discovery.

The miracle of a new life coming into existence, of its becoming a viable part of reality, can never be apprehended by the thoughts in our brains. This is the case whether that new life is a child or a vital work of art. Once the impregnation has happened, the artist, like the woman who is in a family way, will have to accept his subservient role in the process. This acceptance is the art of adapting to reality as the on-going process of life itself, which is founded on mystery.

Just as the mother-to-be feels overtaken and engulfed by the mystery that life is a reality bigger than who we are as individuals, so the artist feels himself drawn into and "incorporated" into the depths of his feeling life where the actuality of "what is realized by all men in common" lives as the intuition guiding his inspiration. In suffering, or allowing, the reality of these deep life-forces to overtake him, the artist transcends the limitation of his work being in any sense merely an egotistical performance of the intellect. By this acceptance, the artist actually contacts reality. By living in, as well as with it, the artist resolves the dilemma of his creation being only the inoculation of the world with his private sickness.

When Dylan drew Ginsberg's attention to Miller's thought about "inoculation," he was reminding Ginsberg about this profound dilemma for the conscience of the artist. Dylan went on immediately to say, "It's not good enough to be an observer all the time. You have to know that you've stopped time. You think about nothing. You're totally absorbed in what you are doing."

In the cyber city of the 20th Century, a good deal that passes for art operates on the principle that the artist is a kind of mirror. The artist, as an exceptionally sensitive and astute observer, mainly records his idiosyncratic impressions so that his art hardly ever transcends being anything more than an eccentric reproduction or imitation of nature, or the world around him. In Dylan's view that is not good enough. The artist has to *know* that he has stopped time, that he has made contact with reality, that he has become a part of that mystery of "what is realized by all men in common."

Like Miller, Dylan recognizes that the solution to this dilemma resides in "letting go," in the artist's free acceptance of his subservient role in the *life process* of creation. In saying that we have to "exist in the moment, so strong as to stop time," Dylan is pointing to what Miller had said, that the artist "has to make himself a part of the mystery, live in as well as with it." This "letting go," this "acceptance," is the art by which contact with reality is made, and for the artist, "that is the great discovery."

The artist, in stopping time, makes contact with reality. In the depths of consciousness beyond time, he connects with the heart of life, where that which "is realized by all men in common" constitutes the source of living intuitions that have the power to imaginatively unify the world. By accepting his subservient role in the creative process, the artist transcends egocentricity, so that his inspirations are guided by those living intuitions rather than by his personal desires. The work of art that comes to birth, as an embodiment of a living intuition, brings new life into the world as a new and fresh insight that can counteract "the loss of general health." In the theory that life is for the education of man, the genius who accomplishes

Coda: Lifting The Veil (If Only A Little)

the heroic feat of stopping time is essential for preserving the general health of human culture.

For Dylan, stopping time was the proof in the pudding, the required confirmation of his art. When you stop time you live in, as well as with, the mystery, and you divine the great secret. Emerson also spoke of this secret:

> It is a secret which every intellectual man quickly learns, that beyond the energy of his possessed and conscious intellect he is capable of a new energy (as of an intellect doubled on itself), by abandonment to the nature of things; that besides his privacy of power as an individual man, there is a great public power on which he can draw, by unlocking, at all risks, his human doors, and suffering the ethereal tides to roll and circulate through him; then he is caught up into the life of the Universe, his speech is thunder, his thought is law, and his words are universally intelligible ....

Stopping time is being "caught up into the life of the Universe." You begin to sense the extremities of your eternal being in much the same way you are able to sense your toes and fingers with your eyes closed. When you succeed in stopping time, you stand present in the moment, which is neither a part of the past nor a part of the future. In the present moment, you merge vertically into eternity and there behold mysteries. You see into the depths beyond this life in the world.

You see, for instance, that at the heart of life in this world there is always a deep wisdom active wherever there is life. You see further that love, always and only born of freedom, is stationed deep within this wisdom. And beyond that even, you see the free being, radiant as ever, pouring forth the wisdom of his love in the light. It is part of the wisdom of life, and of the wisdom of eternal being, that love shall ignite the light.

You see *how* in this world, where we have come to know life, wisdom is the actual foundation of it. In order for even the tiniest form of life to manifest in matter, the collective forces of the entire universe must be called into play, in a manner specific to its outer form. No organism is ever an organization of parts, it is an embodiment of the wisdom underlying all life. Any living organism necessarily implies the whole universe. The mechanical intellectuality of the human brain can not be expected to grapple with, or hope to control, this enormous interplay of cosmic life forces – other than to recognize it and honor it.

In the Bible it is said that the entrance to paradise is guarded by a Cherubim whose sword turns every which way. The mysteries of life can not be apprehended by the brain. They can be known, however, in a certain sense. They can come to light and stand revealed through the intensification of life itself, within the mind of anyone who dares to realize that he *is*, anyone who has come to know himself as *real*. The revelations pertaining to the mysteries of life can only be incorporated into the being of a person who has come to see that this world *where we have come to know life by knowing death*, is actually and vitally imbued with wisdom, that all living forms are saturated with it in a way that is beyond the power of the mind to comprehend.

We need to find the delete button on our brain and dump all the useless files we have accumulated in our mad efforts to understand life. We should know by now that our efforts to understand life have been motivated by the desire to control life. This subtle lust for power lurks even beneath the string theory of those scientists who are searching frantically for the theory of everything. Peel back their quasi-poetic Elegant Universe, and you will see it there, too.

How could we ever hope to understand life with our brains when it is life that *under-stands* us, founding us on mystery? If we had sense enough to approach the altar of the Wisdom underlying life, we would be able to sing along with Walt Whitman that, "The smallest sprout shows there is no death."

And we would know that when we die, we but reenter the world that came before this one. It was there in that earlier world that we had learned the wisdom that presently underlies our being and is currently sustaining this world where we are now living. And like that, we are presently learning that power of love which will become the basis and foundation of the next world. We didn't learn that wisdom, which is the foundation of this world, with our brains – there were not as yet any brains to be had. We learned it with our hearts, with our actual being, even as we are undergoing the same kind of strenuous "learning" of Love here in this world.

The longer we go on playing mind games with our brains, the more foreign this world is bound to become. The more virtual our reality becomes, the less virtuous we are likely to be. Eventually, we will become completely estranged from ourselves. And worst of all, the more foreign this world becomes, the more difficult will be our passing out of it and back into the previous world. At death, when we find ourselves suddenly bodiless again, back in the World of Wisdom, we will have to struggle with might and main to regain our lost orientation to original being – to our "Ever-Present Origin," to use Jean Gebser's words. We will have to re-learn or regain our lost wisdom before it will be possible for us to move on to an experience of love as that power which turns on the light shining in upon us from our future world.

We have come into this world in order to know life by knowing death, because that is the only way really to learn love – not with our brains but with our beings.

Every man alive knows that, despite being alive, he is not himself exempt from death. He shares this much with every other man alive. If he did not himself have to face death, he might easily succeed in living out his whole life unconcerned about "the other." The fate of all others could easily remain a matter of indifference to him.

The purpose of our life here in the world is education, the learning of love and compassion. Our life in the world will always remain only a half-life until we have learned to love "the other." All human beings address themselves by the same name, "I," and we will have to learn to love others as ourselves because in fact they are ourselves. They are other, alternative versions of the same existential self, which is identical in each of us. The existential self is metaphysically a comprehensive being incorporating all who know "I am" – in whom we all live and move and have our being. That comprehensive spiritual self is the actual basis of our I-consciousness. Once love has been "learned" – that is, absorbed into our very being – it will become possible to know the peace that Dylan was talking about when he sang in "Changing Of The Guards" that:

> Peace will come
> With tranquillity and splendor on the wheels
> of fire
> But will bring no reward when her false idols
> fall
> And cruel death surrenders with its pale ghost
> retreating
> Between the King and the Queen of Swords

Coda: Lifting The Veil (If Only A Little)

The falsity of the idols of peace, such as the idea of mundane political tranquility aimed only at ensuring and promoting commerce and trade for the sake of economic capitalism, will be seen to offer no real reward. The peace that will come with the changing of the guards, as the peace that passes all mere intellectualizing, will remove the cruel sting of death to reveal a life beyond. It will be possible to know the tree of life, as he did, when he sang in "Death is Not the End":

> Oh, the tree of life is growing
> Where the spirit never dies
> And the bright light of salvation shines
> In dark and empty skies

As he told Silvio, in the song by that name, Dylan had to go find out something only dead men know.

When the freedom of the unanchored imagination is hit up merely for the talents that can be easily coined into money, due to the proliferation and domination of mass markets, you end up with the kind of rootless culture we have today. You end up surrounding the minds of the young with reality TV, with Survivor and Fear Factor impressions of life which, if the analogy of "inoculating the world with the virus of disillusionment" were taken seriously, would amount to a dangerous metaphor for biological terrorism. What goes on in the world, it seems, is that which lives in the heart of man, whether he would like to know about it or not.

The operation of genius within the artist brings with it, as Emerson said, "the hope and the promise of insight" for the education of man. This "hope and promise" is the source of that "general health" that is lost when genius is sacrificed to talent. Insight is what comes through the artist when he has stopped time, and this influx of insight for the education of man is the source of hope. The insight is for the education of man, but the experience of the eternal in the moment is what augments life for the artist and brings him into contact with reality. This contact is what removes him from "that insidious death," as Miller called it, "which seems to triumph all about him."

Later in the interview with Ginsberg, Dylan says, "You're standing in awe in front of the painting the painter has achieved. Through the art lies immortality. That makes him high, gives him everything he needs, just knowing he can do that." My feeling is that Dylan and Ginsberg had two different ideas of immortality in mind. I think Dylan was trying to suggest to Ginsberg that immortality for the artist himself resides more in the fact that he has stopped time, or experienced the eternal through the creative process, than in the fact that others might continue to be awed by his work for years yet to come. Trying to explain this, Dylan told Ginsberg, "The artist couldn't care less about who sees it." It seems to me that Dylan suddenly realized that Ginsberg's idea of immortality was the conventional one of longevity of fame attached to the work and that Ginsberg was missing the point, that he didn't really understand what Dylan was trying to say. In any case, Dylan paused and then went on to say something that apparently caught Ginsberg by surprise:

> I don't think you're a conscious artist, Allen.
> I don't think you know what you're doing.
> Anybody can be an unconscious artist – I am a conscious artist.

One imagines that Ginsberg may have felt the sting of an accusation, and he responded, "What do you mean I'm not a conscious artist? Are you a conscious artist?" Dylan answered,

Coda: Lifting The Veil (If Only A Little)

"Yes. Because I had a teacher that was a conscious artist, and he drilled it into me to be a conscious artist."

Dylan's interview with Ginsberg took place in September of 1977. One year later, shortly after the release of his *Street Legal* album, Dylan would be interviewed again, this time by Jonathan Cott, for *Rolling Stone* magazine. In this interview he offered some more thoughts about himself as a *conscious artist*. Referring to the images and themes of his *Street Legal* album, he said:

> These are things I'm really interested in, and it's taken me a while to get back to it. Right through the time of *Blonde on Blonde* I was doing it unconsciously. Then one day I was half-stepping, and the lights went out. And since that point, I more or less had amnesia. Now, you can take that statement as literally or metaphorically as you need to, but that's what happened to me. It took me a long time to get to do consciously what I used to do unconsciously.

Dylan went on to explain to Cott, "So now I'm connected back, and I don't know how long I'll be there because I don't know how long I'm going to live. But what comes now is for real and from a place that's ... I don't know, I don't care who else cares about it."

For Miller, the great discovery for the artist was that through art "one finally establishes contact with reality." When Dylan said to Cott, "But what comes now is for real and from a place that's ...," he couldn't quite finish the statement.

One may not announce to another that "I have made contact with reality" and expect it to mean anything to him. It is simply an experience too intense and profound for expression in ordinary language. In the "contact with reality," the personal "I" itself, for all intents and purposes, dissolves into the "All-I," to use Steiner's expression.

So such a statement would be bound to ring false, first of all in the ears of the one making it. The emotional intensity of this inner paradox was well captured by Dylan in "Something There Is About You," in the following lines: "I could say that I'd be faithful, I could say it in one sweet easy breath/But to you that would be cruelty and to me it surely would be death." So intimate is the contact with reality that as soon as it is uttered by the personal "I," the contact is broken, and the statement becomes false.

All the artist can do, *as artist*, is trust in the process that brings his art into being. In the quickening of life, in stopping time, he sees, and he knows (in the sense of gnosis), and he creates. Living in and with the mystery, he can only trust that his creation, however awkward or inadequate it may appear to some, will nevertheless possess real healing powers for those who are open to it. In that way, it will contribute to the general health of culture.

With his heart attuned to the quickening of life over and above any desire for success, he is able to deliver, like the pregnant woman, a new embodiment of life. Caught up into the life of the Universe, he submits himself to that greater power. Living in and with the mystery, he consciously serves it, lending his forces and talents to its purposes.

From Dylan's statements to Cott, it would appear that in some sense the *Street Legal* album marks the transition for Dylan from unconscious to conscious artist. This album, amazingly recorded in only one week between the legs of a world tour, is perhaps the most esoteric of Dylan's albums. It established the initiatory basis for the transformation that led to his so-called Christian period. It is a convincing demonstration that what

Coda: Lifting The Veil (If Only A Little)

he was doing unconsciously up to *Blonde on Blonde* had now become very conscious indeed.

But what is it that Dylan has been doing, either consciously or unconsciously, for all these years? The best description of Dylan's special kind of art is to be found, I believe, in an early book of Martin Buber's, called *DANIEL*, which has the subtitle, "Dialogues On Realization." This was an early book by Buber, published in 1913. Obviously, then, this is not a book *about* Dylan. It is, however, a book about the kind of inward questing for spiritual reality that remains the hallmark of Dylan's work. The book is comprised of five dialogues between Daniel, a sort of sage-persona, with various others. These five dialogues are listed in the table of contents like this:

> On Direction. Dialogue in the Mountains
> On Reality. Dialogue Above the City
> On Meaning. Dialogue in the Garden
> On Polarity. Dialogue After the Theater
> On Unity. Dialogue by the Sea

The first chapter, "On Direction," is a short, mystical conversation between Daniel and "the Woman." Anyone who has come to the point of interpreting Dylan's songs as I have been doing in this book will certainly find this chapter of interest. However, the amazingly accurate and point-by-point description of how Dylan's art really works is to be found in the second chapter, "On Reality." Daniel and his companion, Ulrich, have just returned from a sojourn in the city when they begin their conversation.

> *Ulrich*: How the voices of the city die away! Only in this small stretch have we wandered from them, and already all their noise, which

> even now spurted up to us, has fallen into the great mixing bowl of distance, and of all the storms of its haste this rustle remains with us — almost a song.
>
> *Daniel*: A song, Ulrich, a song! Yes, they tugged and shrieked like sick hounds on the chain, the goal-possessed thousand-times-thousand; they raged against and through one another, and still there throbbed unknown in each throat the longing for the song that is liberated now not in their ears but in ours. There was a moment when I heard it otherwise: in the midst of the tumult of the street, not a play of the distance, but the bleeding nearness, sung to me by the longing of the longing ones.
>
> *Ulrich*: One moment?

For Ulrich the storms of haste from the city below rustle up to them almost like a song. For Daniel, it is not only *like* a song, it is a song. It is a song, which he has heard in two different ways. Once when it was "liberated" in their ears through their conversation, as they recalled the shrieking of the goal-possessed many. And, originally, in a single moment of bleeding nearness while they had been going among those longing ones in the tumult of the streets. The song he heard in that moment was the song as it was sung to him by "the longing of the longing ones." What surprises Ulrich is that Daniel had heard it all in a moment.

Coda: Lifting The Veil (If Only A Little)

> *Daniel*: Do you not know what the moment which you allow to fulfill itself brings you, what a flood of song and light?

Well, here we are again. The "moment which you allow to fulfill itself" sounds an awful lot like "existing so strong in the moment," as Dylan put it, "that you stop time." Such a strong abiding in the moment becomes a "timeless" moment when you are flooded with "song and light." In other words, such an intense experience of the present moment becomes impersonally, or rather supra-personally, cognitive. When the personal "I" dissolves into the "All-I," it doesn't cease to exist as such. By becoming still, it is no longer an obstruction, and life quickens into the song and light of inspiration. Daniel goes on to tell Ulrich what he experienced in that moment.

> I went among the crowd and thought of nothing other than opening my soul so wide to it, so to unbolt granary and treasure house that everything might find place in it of the open and hidden need of these men of which I could in any way be aware. I spoke within myself: What can I do for you, you who rush around me without purpose and touch me without understanding, nameless crowd?

The song of longing, the longing of the longing ones, of the goal-possessed hordes, awakens in Daniel a deep compassion for those lost in the tumult of the streets of the city. In the quickening of life, in the blissful experience of "contact with reality," all identities merge and fuse.

In the timeless moment when the personal "I" all but dissolves, the artist knows, perhaps better than anyone else, that even with all his many talents he is hardly distinguishable from any other human being. When the inspiration is conceived in him, the augmentation of life that overtakes him humbles him. He knows that he is not the source, but only the agent, and that in and of himself he is no different than any other. So profound, so indelible, is this experience that the true artist can do no other than feel himself one with even the lowest and the most lost.

This is what prompted Henry Miller, after making his point about "what is realized by all men in common," to recognize that this deep experience of compassion is what gives any idea or principle its validity. He went on to say that:

> People are always worried about the fate of the genius. I never worried about the genius: genius takes care of the genius in man. My concern was always for the nobody, the man who is lost in the shuffle, the man who is so common, so ordinary, that his presence is not even noticed.

Such compassion is always at the heart of great art. It permeates Dylan's whole body of work, but is perhaps no more evident than in "Chimes of Freedom" where he sings "for every hung-up person in the whole wide universe."

In "the moment" when Daniel heard "the song" in its "bleeding nearness," it was a song born of compassion in which he felt his life one with all of "the longing ones." He goes on to tell Ulrich what that quickening of life brought him to understand about his relation to the longing ones:

> I have not the power to heal you and have not
> the art to comfort you; and if I sacrifice my life

Coda: Lifting The Veil (If Only A Little)

for you, nothing would be accomplished. But this I may do: receive you, gather your scattered pain in me, make your torn pieces whole in me, so that my soul may become your song, you songless one.

In this description of Daniel's great compassion, there is an accurate picture of Dylan's special art and calling. His function, as artist, has been this ineffable opening of himself to us in deepest compassion, and with the profoundest humility to receive the torn pieces of our scattered pain, making it whole in himself and allowing his soul to become *our* song. In a certain sense, this could be said of any great poet or artist. Dylan, however, seems to have been clearly conscious of the sacred nature of this special calling, specially after *Blonde On Blonde*.

Consider, for instance, what Dylan told Mikal Gilmore, who interviewed him for the September 22, 2001 issue of *Rolling Stone* magazine. While Dylan was answering a question about the album, *"Love and Theft,"* which had been released coincidentally on September 11, 2001, Dylan finished his response with the following aside:

> ... just to make another record at this point in my career ... career, by the way, isn't how I look at what I do. *Career* is a French word. It means "carrier." It's something that takes you from one place to another. I don't feel like what I do qualifies to be called a career. It's more of a calling.

As I see it, it was Dylan's calling to enter the spiritual chaos of the 20th Century, this cyber city that continues to hold us within its walls, in much the same way that Daniel had gone among the crowd of the city. Like Daniel, he has been moved by the deepest compassion. Even the shape his "career" had taken, as the years went by, seems analogous to Daniel's experience:

> And with this will I went through the crowd. And then this will became actual in me; it happened to me, so that I no longer knew myself but only a tumult of forces, hitting and rushing past one another without measure or way. But in the center of the tumult a heart dwelt, like a human heart, which received blood from the whirl and sent it again to all its corners. And the presence of this formless and unruly body at first so overpowered me that I performed my service like a pump, humble and stupefied. But then meaning came over me again, and I received from each of these forces, yes, from each of these galloping, purpose-mad forces – from the hungry and the greedy, from the seeking and the grasping – rising from each, I received a song.

The parallel is uncanny. One can easily imagine that Dylan, too, after entering the tumult of the 20th Century, eventually became aware of something like a human heart beating at the center of the swirl that spurred him on to perform his service, unconsciously at first, like a pump. By the by, Dylan would come to give that human-like heart the ancient name of "Christ," and many would jump to the banal conclusion that Dylan had suddenly got religion. But let's go a little further with Daniel:

Coda: Lifting The Veil (If Only A Little)

> O that pale, flickering, ghostlike singing! As I received it, I became fainthearted, my friend, fainthearted with choking compassion, and no longer had any will in me other than this one – to be again a man and to take one of these men by the hand and say to him: "Remember, brother, that your soul is a free and mighty firmament that nothing can compel." Then I threw off and abjured my office, and already I stood again in my body, in the midst of the crowd. But I did so trembling and saw what was around me as a gigantic circling top, and my lips were struck dumb. Thus I stood trembling and mute, and after I had stood awhile, I went home and sat on a bench in the garden and was alone in worse loneliness than ever before ...
>
> Only much later, however, was it revealed to me what I had known in that moment.
>
> *Ulrich*: In that moment? How can you be so certain of that?

And so here we are back to that moment, which we allow to fulfill itself, the present moment in which time stops, when the soul of the artist is caught up in the ecstasy of the quickening life of the universe. The epitome of this experience is the need to take a man by the hand and say to him, "Remember, brother, that your soul is a free and mighty firmament that nothing can compel." But the intensity of this experience is too much, too powerful, and one wants to return to the human state. There, one lives with this knowledge, this gnosis, in extreme loneliness, until all you had known in that moment becomes gradually revealed.

"In that moment?" Ulrich says. "How can you be so certain of that?" Daniel tries to explain:

> You know certainly about what is called the sign in an act of knowing. You wake up one morning or you pause on a walk and you have a thought in your hands, a knowing thought that you see for the first time and yet which is as ripe and ready as if you had formed it over a very long time. But while you are regarding it, you notice that it bears a sign: it is an image out of a place and a moment and in it the seal of a life-experience. And whether you establish your knowledge in the holiness of silence or offer it for sale on the market of words, the sign cleaves to it.

What is this but an astonishingly precise description of how gnosis and inspiration operate? When the act of knowing revisits you in an image that rings true, not because it is a bright idea, but because it is vibrant with the seal of your own life experience, you see it again for the first time. Now it is supercharged with all its many-faceted meanings. You know what you know, not from brain-generated thoughts, but from the intrinsic interconnectedness of all that confirms your life. The sign in the act of knowing is the point where your life sparks with the life of the universe.

This knowledge, this gnosis, belongs to you as the confirmation of your eternal nature. It is holy, whether you hold it in silence or publish it "on the market of words." It doesn't require external proof of its truth and reality. If you do offer

Coda: Lifting The Veil (If Only A Little)

it for sale, the sign will cleave to it. Those who respond to it will recognize, even if they don't realize it, that you have stopped time.

> *Ulrich*: And perhaps it is this that allows us to feel our knowledge as something living and indestructible even when it is preserved in silence ... But what was it, Daniel, that you knew at that time?
>
> *Daniel*: If I may say it to you as simply as I knew it: he remains unreal who does not realize.

We remain unreal until we realize. This may be what Dylan meant when he said, "When it resolves itself, it's never resolved – you have to resolve it. To resolve is nothing more than letting go." Possibly Dylan was thinking here of Miller's words:

> The world has not to be put in order: the world is order incarnate. It is for us to put ourselves in unison with this order, to know what is the world order in contradistinction to the wishful-thinking orders which we seek to impose on one another. The power which we long to possess, in order to establish the good, the true and the beautiful, would prove to be, if we could have it, but the means of destroying one another. It is fortunate that we are powerless. We have first to acquire vision, then discipline and forbearance. Until we have the humility to acknowledge the existence of a vision beyond our own, until we have faith and

trust in superior powers, the blind must lead the blind. The men who believe that work and brains will accomplish everything must ever be deceived by the quixotic and unforeseen turn of events. They are the ones who are perpetually disappointed; no longer able to blame the gods, or God, they turn on their fellow-men and vent their impotent rage by crying "Treason! Stupidity!" and other hollow terms.

Like Daniel in his "Dialogue above the City," Dylan came down into the city of the 20th Century, going among the goal-possessed thousand-times-thousand as they raged against and through one another. They are raging still. We have seen how he has opened himself and heard the song of the longing ones, and how, as artist, he has made their scattered pain whole again, letting his soul become their song. Only now, in the great mixing bowl of distance – in that preternatural distance that separates frozen time from the eternal moment – is that song to be liberated.

It should be noted that Robert Shelton, in his biography of Dylan, *No Direction Home*, tells us that already in 1965 Albert Grossman, who was Dylan's manager at the time, had given Dylan several of Martin Buber's books. He doesn't say which books, but he does say that, "During his retreat, Dylan read Buber, mused sullenly, wrote like a floodtide."

DISCOGRAPHY

Songs By Bob Dylan Discussed In Their Entirety:

"All Along the Watchtower," *John Wesley Harding*, 1968.
"Black Diamond Bay," *Desire*, 1975.
"Bob Dylan's Blues," *The Freewheelin' Bob Dylan*, 1963.
"Changing of the Guards," *Street Legal*, 1978.
"Dark Eyes," *Empire Burlesque*, 1985.
"Eternal Circle," *Bootleg Series, vols. 1-3*, 1991.
"Golden Loom," *Bootleg Series, vols. 1-3*, 1991.
"I and I," *Infidels*, 1983.
"I Shall Be Released," *Bob Dylan's Greatest Hits, vol. II*, 1971.
"I Want You," *Blonde On Blonde*, 1966.
"Isis," *Desire*, 1975.
"Jokerman," *Infidels* 1983.
"Just Like A Woman," *Blonde On Blonde*, 1966.
"Like A Rolling Stone," *Highway 61 Revisited*, 1965.
"Precious Angel," *Slow Train Coming*, 1979.
"Pressing On," *Saved*, 1980.
"Saving Grace," *Saved*, 1980.
"Señor (Tales of Yankee Power)," *Street Legal*, 1978.
"Shelter From The Storm," *Blood On The Tracks*, 1974.
"Visions of Johanna," *Blonde On Blonde*, 1966.
"Where Are You Tonight? (Journey Through Dark Heat)," *Street Legal*, 1978.
"You're a Big Girl Now," *Blood On The Tracks*, 1974.

SELECTED BIBLIOGRAPHY

Books Quoted in Text.

Allen, Paul M, *Vladimir Soloviev, Russian Mystic*, Rudolf Steiner Publications, New York, 1973.

Auden, W. H., *The Collected Poetry of W. H. Auden*, Random House, New York, 1945.

Bauldie, John, editor, *Wanted Man: In Search of Bob Dylan*, Citadel Press, New York, 1991.

Berdyaev, Nicolas, *Dostoevsky*, The World Publishing Co., Cleveland and New York, 1957.

Berdyaev, Nicolas, *The Beginning & The End*, Harper & Brothers, New York, 1957.

Briffault, Robert, *The Troubadours*, Indiana University Press, Bloomington, 1965.

Buber, Martin, *Daniel, Dialogues On Realization*, translated By Maurice Friedman, Holt, Rinehart and Winston, New York, 1964.

Dylan, Bob, *Lyrics 1962-2001*, Simon & Schuster, New York, 2004.

Eckhart, Johannes, *Meister Eckhart*, Harper & Row, New York, 1941.

Eliot, T. S., *Uses Of Poetry And Uses Of Criticism*, Harvard University Press, 1933.

Emerson, Ralph Waldo, *The Works Of Ralph Waldo Emerson*, Blacks Reader Svc., Roslyn, New York, undated.

Emerson, Ralph Waldo, *Natural History Of The Intellect*, Solar Press, New York, 1995.

Emerson, Ralph Waldo, *Essays And Journals*, Communications And Studies, Inc., Atlanta, 1968.

Hesse, Hermann, *My Belief*, Farrar, Straus and Giroux, New York, 1974.

Miller, Henry, *The World Of Sex*, Grove Press, Inc., New York, 1965.

Miller, Henry, *Sexus*, Grove Press, Inc., New York, 1965.

Shelton, Robert, *No Direction Home, The Life and Music of Bob Dylan*, Ballantine Books, New York, 1986.

Soloviev, Vladimir, *Lectures on Godmanhood*, Dobson Books, England, 1981.

Soloviev, Vladimir, *God, Man and Church: The Spiritual Foundation of Life*, Attic Press, Greenwood, SC, 1975.

Steiner, Rudolf, *Background to the Gospel of St. Mark*, Rudolf Steiner Press, London, 1968.

Steiner, Rudolf, *Cosmic Memory*, Rudolf Steiner Publications, New York, 1971.

Steiner, Rudolf, *Eleven European Mystics*, Rudolf Steiner Publications, New York, 1971.

Tagore, Rabindranath, *Personality*, McMillan Press, New York, 1917.

Thompson, William Irwin, *Darkness and Scattered Light*, Anchor Books, 1978.

Thompson, William Irwin, *The Time Falling Bodies Take To Light*, St. Martin's Press, New York, 1981.

Whitman, Walt, *Leaves Of Grass, The First (1855) Edition*, The Viking Press, New York, 1959.

Yeats, William Butler, *The Autobiography of William Butler Yeats*, Collier, New York, 1967.

www.ingramcontent.com/pod-product-compliance
Lightning Source LLC
Chambersburg PA
CBHW031948080426
42735CB00007B/311